"Lots of people are fed up with 'organized religion.' They recognized that religion is too often poorly organized–or well-organized around the wrong purposes! That's why this book is so valuable: drawing wisdom from the important field of community organizing, it helps you imagine a church organizing well and for the right purposes."

   – Brian D. McLaren, activist, author of *The Great Spiritual Migration*

"Tim Conder and Dan Rhodes know what they are talking about. They have formed and reformed a number of congregations and have been leaders in fitting churches for more faithful, fruitful futures. Now they tell us how in their spirited call for churches to organize themselves to make a more vibrant Christian witness in their communities. They make a strong case that in giving to our community contexts we receive more lively, faithful congregations. Conder and Rhodes have led community organizing ministry in their contexts, now they guide us in organizing the church Christ means for us to be."

   – Will Willimon, Duke Divinity School, United Methodist Bishop (retired)

"J. I. Packer once observed that the problem of evangelical and free churches is they suffer from a 'stunted ecclesiology.' If his diagnosis was correct, and I believe it was, then Conder and Rhodes offer the equivalent of an ecclesial growth hormone therapy. The ecclesiology they propose begins at the level of practice and moves to theological reflection. This book should be at the top of the list for anyone seeking to understand what it means for congregations to be the Body of Christ's continuing presence in the world."

   – Curtis W. Freeman, Duke University Divinity School, author of *Contesting Catholicity* and *Undomesticated Dissent.*

"This book doesn't allow us to whine about what's wrong in the world or the church: it is a bold and prophetic call to practical actions of compassion and conviction. It can serve as a field guide to re-envision the church as a neighbor who both loves and practices compassion but it is a bold and prophetic call to both reflective and decisive engagement as artists who fearlessly craft something beautiful in ordinary and familiar neighborhoods in your town and mine. What the reader cannot do is to remain disengaged from the agency of activism in the life of the Body of Christ....Belief without practice is an abstract exercise which brings little value or change. Practice without belief is an exercise in subjectivity and randomness. Conder and Rhodes have written a call to belief and practice in an ancient form that they call Organizing the Church. The early church practiced it as apostolic ministry–forming communities of faith and practice grounded in time and place in particular cultures."

   – Keith R. Anderson, President, Seattle School of Theology & Psychology and author of *A Spirituality of Listening* and *Reading Your Life's Story: An Invitation to Spiritual Mentoring*

"You think you have heard about white evangelicals in politics. But have you heard this other (very different) story that Conder and Rhodes tell? One of congregations organizing for justice with black and brown sisters and brothers, learning from the IAF and the NAACP, working for justice for all people and creation, participating in bringing the kingdom Jesus preached? The former might win you the White House. But the latter is bigger and more lasting–it points to--no, it *is*–the Beloved Community. This book is brimming with grace and wisdom and hard work and good cheer."

   – Jason Byassee, Vancouver School of Theology

"The Church is badly in need of an ecclesiology which is world centered and not self centered. Organizing needs to remake itself for the new world we find ourselves in. Articulating a theology of our situation is the starting point. *Organizing Church* is a contribution to both needs. If we learn from it, we can provide hope and bread for a world in turmoil."

> – Gerald Kellman, Reinvestment Organizer and Barack Obama's organizing mentor

"A very timely book! Tim and Dan invite you down a path that's, as they describe, not for the faint of heart or the dull of spirit. They include thoroughly researched organizational practices to help along your journey."

> – Vanna Fox, Senior Vice President, Wild Goose Festival

"In a season of fearful speculation about what the future holds for the Church, I believe more than anything that the future belongs to churches who have deep relationships, strong local commitments, and a community ethic of working toward a beloved community. In other words, I believe the future of the church belongs to churches like Tim's, churches you will likely never hear about who do the quiet work, day in and day out, of faithful discipleship. Many pastors and faith communities *want* to be this kind of church; most don't know how. This book is for them. With clarity of vision and a plethora of practical applications, *Organizing Church* will guide your congregation toward being an active participant in both personal and communal transformation in your community. I highly recommend this book to pastors, lay leaders, and all followers of Jesus who are looking to reexamine their understanding of church and reclaim its prophetic and transformative role in society."

> – Danielle Shroyer, author, speaker, pastor

Organizing
CHURCH

Organizing CHURCH

*Grassroots Practices for
Embodying Change
In Your Congregation,
Your Community,
and Our World*

TIM CONDER

DAN RHODES

chalice press

Saint Louis, Missouri

An imprint of Christian Board of Publication

ChalicePress.com

Print: 9780827227637
EPUB: 9780827227644   EPDF: 9780827227651

Printed in the United States of Anerica

CONTENTS

Acknowledgments   xi

1 **RE**-ASSESSING the Church
   as It Is and Could Be   1

2 **RE**-DEFINING the Church:
   Practice-Based Ecclesiology   12

3 **RE**-EMPOWERING the Church:
   Why Power Matters for Congregations   29

4 **RE**-CONNECTING the Church:
   The Constructive Practice of the
   Relational Meeting   46

5 **RE**-COLLECTING the Church:
   House Meetings and Discernment   63

6 **RE**-UNITING the Church:
   On Conflict and Revitalization   78

7 **RE**-DISCOVERING the Church:
   An Organizing and Reorganizing
   Community   98

   Appendix 1: One-to-Ones   112

   Appendix 2: House Meetings/
   Listening Sessions   116

   Notes   118

Acknowledgments

The Organizers

By its nature, community organizing is collaborative, and this book would not have been possible without the wisdom, input, training, and examples of our colleagues and mentors in the Metro Industrial Areas Foundation (IAF). We want to particularly thank the IAF organizers of the Southeast and North Carolina United Power and Durham Congregations, Associations, and Neighborhoods (CAN), who have patiently worked with us for many years. This begins with the current lead organizer of Durham CAN, Ivan Parra, who largely introduced us to many of these practices by seeking us out for relational meetings long before we had heard that term used. Gerald Taylor, a now-retired IAF regional organizer, has been a mentor who has told us both more meaningful stories and given us more memorable quotes than we could ever report. Gerald always led with a deep insistence of a relational culture and fought tirelessly to maintain that culture. We have been deeply impacted by that example. He has been a warrior for justice on so many fronts, but has always made time for us. We also want to attribute a great deal of this wisdom to our current regional organizer, Martin Trimble. Martin's presentation of the relational meeting (which we relied on in chapter four) at IAF's National Training in 2015 was clear, enriched by the wise stories of decades of organizing, and immediately actionable. Additionally, we would like to thank Mike Gecan, whose training materials on congregational development provided something of a backdrop for the structure and argument of chapter six. And we would like to profusely thank our colleagues in Durham CAN's Clergy Caucus, including Rev. Dr. Herb Davis,

Bishop Clarence Laney, Rev. Dr. Mike Broadway, and Rev. Mark Anthony-Middleton. Particularly those four have been brothers in the struggle for over a decade. It has been a privilege to follow their lead, and we are thankful for the number times that they have had our back.

I (Tim) would also like to thank the leadership of the North Carolina's NAACP's "Forward Together" Moral Movement. Their example of using a broad-based ecumenical theology as impetus for organizing has been inspiring to us and has moved many thousands of people in North Carolina to organize, work, and protest for justice in our state. Rev. Dr. William Barber II is a gifted, generous, prophetic leader with a passionate message of hope that all people of faith and moral ethic should hear. I also want to specifically thank Rev. Dr. Rodney Sadler and Bishop Tonyia Rawls for their tremendous examples in pastoral ministry, organizing leadership, and theological vision. They have shared reams of great advice with me that has been transformative in my own efforts to lead and organize. Rev. Steve Knight has been a friend and colleague for decades. I have been honored to organize, stand, and "jail" with him in this movement. David LaMotte has also profoundly impacted my understanding of organizing people of faith. His gifts as a justice leader and artist are immense. His music beautifully engages and advances the vision of this text.

I (Dan) am extremely grateful for the kindred spirits I've discovered working in a new town. Rev. Kristin White and Rev. Jim Honig have not only shaped my thinking on organizing and its relationship to the church, they have been invaluable instructors and mutual partners in building this connection. I am in great debt to their insights and to their tireless work, for without them and other ministers like them this book would make no sense. I would also like to thank Fernando Rayas and Fr. Gary Graf, whose current work to envision and develop a new apostolate program for young adults through the emerging Parish Peace Project provides a true image of what an organizing church can be.

Our Community

Our ministry lives also have been overwhelmed by a beautiful collaboration with the leaders of Emmaus Way, an activist and organizing congregation that we had the privilege to pastor together for almost a decade. Emmaus Way is truly an organic community where everyone leads. So many friends, including those who challenged us, have made a profound impact on this book. We are eternally thankful for our lead artists, Wade Baynham and now Mark Williams, who have so powerfully found, written, and performed great musical texts of lament that reframe both hope and justice for our community. Josh Busman and Ben Haas have been our primary liturgists who craft music and other art forms into compelling worship gatherings. We also thoroughly recommend Josh's scholarship in musicology. His dissertation was an ethnographic study of contemporary evangelical worship music that established a strong correlation between the individualism of experience and triumphalism of this dominant, commercial genre of worship music with the social passivity of its consumers! Molly Brummett Wudel joined Emmaus Way as a co-pastor two years ago and has only amplified our commitment to organizing. She read portions of this book and her input as a feminist process theologian was substantive. This text is better because of her critique and affirmation. Our community's lay leaders through the years—including Jenny Nicholson, Dave Efird, Ben Haas, Sarah Kate Fishback, Emily McLean, and Laura Wooten—have been willing to engage, support, and enrich this vision to be an organizing church. We wish every pastor had the privilege to work with leaders and a community like this. Finally, since the writing of this book for me (Dan) has straddled a transition from Durham, North Carolina to Chicago, I would like to thank the congregation of St. Augustine's Episcopal, a community that has not only graciously welcomed my family but continues to refreshingly embody Christ in ways that broaden and strengthen my hope.

Our Families

I (Tim) want to humbly thank my wife, Meredith, and our two adult children, Keenan and Kendall, for their role in this text and gift to my life. We have shared a household where the justice vision of God's kingdom has been the dominant discourse. Each of them has surpassed my own vision with their lives and hopes, and my work has been radically impacted by the gift of sharing life in this family. My Dad, Don Conder, whom I admire so much, has brought a unique gift to my life as an organizing pastor. He is a pragmatist who has always been motivated by common sense, courageous but gentle engagement, and longsuffering kindness. My tone in sometimes very contentious work has been altered and impacted by his legacy of kindness. My brother and sister-in-law, Keenan and Debbie Conder, have been so generous to me and my family. Their support, not the least being providing a beautiful place to write in the midst of my chaotic pastoral/academic life, has been overwhelming. This support has made so many aspects of my work possible. Enduring thanks to all of you!

I (Dan) am boundlessly grateful to my wife, Elizabeth, whose patience, kindness, and enduring hopefulness astound me. I may be the theologian, but you teach me daily what it means to actually embody the gospel. I'd also like to thank my two daughters, Rachel and Julia, whose zest for life and ceaseless love present me with gifts beyond measure. To my parents, David and Debbie, I owe an unlimited debt of gratitude for raising me in the faith and for teaching me what it means to take it seriously. My brother, Dave, has perhaps been my longest dialogue partner, and his collaborative spirit fills these pages. He and his wife, Kim, embody a dedication to the service of the kingdom of God that enlivens my own faith. The compassion of my sister, Kayleigh, and her desire to find the kingdom especially in marginalized others give me hope for the future of the church. Lastly, I want to thank my in-laws, Paul and Libby Sarazen, for the generous way they've opened their home to our family, making it possible for me to write.

All those above have been for us a great cloud of witnesses, embodying a glimpse of the kingdom we seek to promote in *Organizing Church*.

For the community organizers and clergy who have taught us what it means to embody the deeply relational culture of the kingdom.

1

RE-ASSESSING
the Church as It Is and Could Be

It is fair to say that Dan and I have sustained a tumultuous love affair with the church. A complicated but inescapable devotion seems inevitable for us, given that we have had so many personally and professionally formative experiences under the caring and often maddening wings of the church. Sara Groves' achingly beautiful song "The Long Defeat" (2007) has been a favorite in the worship liturgy of the community we led together. It describes the spiritual hopes and struggles of so many in our fellowship, including us. Here are the final lyrics:

> And I pray for inspiration
> And a way I cannot see
> It's too heavy to carry
> And impossible to leave
> It's too heavy to carry
> And I will never leave[1]

We appear to be church lifers. We never intend to leave. But we have prayed for, hoped for, and painfully struggled for new ways forward. Without getting too far ahead of ourselves, here's a snapshot of the backdrop that shapes our difficult devotion to the body of Christ.

The rural Baptist church I (Tim) attended in my childhood was a centerpiece of community life in that small corner of Mecklenburg County, North Carolina, where I grew up. The obvious integrity of so many kind and caring persons, the unchangeable routines, the unshakable doctrine, and celebratory funerals—even the casseroles, softball games, and wild play with the other kids on the

1

grounds—yielded a rooted sense of safety that certainly trumped the long sermons, the unquestioned expectation of dressing up, and my parents' insistence that we attend three times a week (Sunday mornings, Sunday evenings, and Wednesday nights!). I grew up about as "churched" as you can get. I made it to my teens before my innocent assent began to erode. Dan's roots are remarkably similar, another Baptist (in his case Independent Baptist) living in the deep South—though he one-ups my story a bit by being a "pastor's kid." Dan was actually born while his father taught at Bob Jones University. As a child and teen, he watched his dad struggle free of the harsh embrace of fundamentalism and preach a hopeful gospel in communities that often seemed to fear change more than they did death. Most of his family remains "in the business," so to speak, serving the church in various roles.

The first church I served during my mid-twenties, while in seminary, was located in Boston's suburban technology belt. This large church had a historical and well-executed commitment to programmatic excellence. Meetings began and ended on time. The stacked VAX superminicomputer in a dedicated air-conditioned room looked like it could run NASA in a pinch, and the brand new, boxy, chunky Macintosh SE's were mobile and absolutely superb! Brochures were sleek and impeccable. The office ran like a Timex is supposed to. The staff was professional. The senior pastor was widely renowned. Sermons were thoughtful, organized, and culturally relevant to the young professionals who filled the pews. Given my humble, blue-collar, country roots, the congregants were oh-so-polished and impressive!

My ecclesial journey continued with many exciting and unforeseen stops. Through long association with The Leadership Network, a foundation in Texas that networked large churches, I was exposed to the deep humanity of staff members at some of the most notable megachurches in the country during the season of their meteoric growth and unchallenged cultural ascent. As a leader in the Emergent Church movement, I encountered and watched the birth of fellowships that were theologically, culturally, artistically, and economically creative beyond my wildest expectations. Though some of these communities grew notably, many were intentionally small and surprisingly beautiful. To that point I had been enchanted by the possibilities of large churches and was often shocked to see the potential of these small communities. In response to that vision, I founded a small Christian community in Durham, North Carolina

(Emmaus Way), that Dan joined in our first year. He and I then pastored together for a decade (and I continue to co-pastor) this artistic, passionate, thoughtful, over-educated, odd, small community that overwhelms us with hope.

Obviously, we have been immersed in low-church Protestantism. But when Dan first attended the church I was planting, he told me we were "free church sacramentalists"—meaning that while our polity and order eschewed hierarchy and pomp, we were a community that no less stressed the real presence of God's grace among us, particularly in our collective practices. Somewhere along the way, I found the wonder and mystery of the Roman Catholic Church and, largely through the influence of Jesuit spirituality, began receiving spiritual direction and developed a growing love for liturgy. I often share that I finally learned to pray, despite all those years in church, when I was guided in the rule of Ignatius of Loyola's Spiritual Exercises. As a Duke Divinity M.Div. and Th.D., finding community in Duke's Baptist House, Dan was schooled in the value of liturgy and institutional structure. Hence, it was no surprise that when Dan finished his degree a few years ago, he followed the call to teach at Loyola University in Chicago and his family found a home in the wonderful community of St. Augustine's Episcopal.

In the last decade, as pastors deeply involved in community organizing and as scholars whose research often engages churches of color, our horizons have been enlarged and our convictions both challenged and strengthened. We have witnessed the might and splendor of the Southern black church, a powerful institution that prompted the legendary Duke University professor and pastor Charles Eric Lincoln to offer this epithet:

> Beyond its purely religious function, as critical as
> that has been, the Black church in its historical
> role as lyceum, conservatory, forum, social service
> center, political academy and financial institution,
> has been and is for Black America the mother of
> our culture, the champion of our freedom, the
> hallmark of our civilization.[2]

We, too, have been captivated by the black church and the many churches of color in our communities who have led the fight for justice and taught us so much about what it means to embody the gospel. We have been honored to engage together for change in our communities.

These political experiences have taken us far from our conservative roots into mainline and progressive congregations: the "liberal" churches we were taught to disregard and even fear in our childhood. Moreover, we've forged strong relationships among neo-monastic communities, other intentional communities, and in the networks of progressive evangelicals. We certainly haven't seen all of the ecclesial landscape and don't pretend to have done so. But simply put, we have a long history of encountering the rich diversity of the church and continue to do so.

Having seen so many great possibilities and beautiful expressions of Christian community, we must admit, however, that we are also profoundly...disappointed. That disappointment in the midst of such great potential was the tension that formed the starting place for this book.

Before naming that disappointment, we want to be quick to distinguish our disappointment from our horror. We are truly horrified (but not surprised) that various streams of Christianity have become integrally entrenched in white privilege, racism, nationalism, xenophobia, nonsensical supports of the Second Amendment, national militarism, anti-intellectual pride/fear that rejects important scientific consensuses, and an unblinkingly idolatrous commitment to capitalism. Having grown up during the nationally prominent desegregation battle in the Charlotte-Mecklenburg school system, I have always known that churches could be wrong on social issues and social change. And I have never forgotten the critical impulse that was forged in the discoveries that shattered my faithful innocence. There is clearly a need for ongoing constructive critique. We also share in the duty to support those who prophetically write about the structural deformation of the church in our present society.[3]

But this book is not about that horror; it is about the possibility we have glimpsed at times in many churches and faith communities—who, when organized, exhibit a beautiful, relational authenticity within their fellowship, and have rallied to do some astounding faithful justice work where they are. In just over a decade in our own community, we have labored with other congregations to secure living wage agreements from our city and the major university that is our city's largest employer. We have fought successfully to establish universal free breakfasts (along with the already established lunch subsidy) for students in need in our public school system. We've worked together to orchestrate one of the most effective rapid-rehousing network resources in the nation. Right now, in a city that is exploding with urban professional growth and the subsequent secondary explosion of development and city subsidies for upper-end housing for the entrepreneurial class (aka TIFs or other tax breaks), we are securing downtown land adjacent to significant transportation hubs for the development of workforce housing for those earning below the median income. Statewide, the NAACP's Moral Movement is leading a coalition that includes an ecumenical and multifaith array of fellowships to fight against a coordinated attack from lawmakers on voting rights, the privatization (and, as we all know, segregation) of public education, and the invidious rejection of Medicaid expansion that results in the deaths of hundreds of North Carolinians each year. As enthusiastic participants/leaders in that coalition, we have pushed for living wages and protecting the environment and have engaged in the struggle for what we take to be kingdom justice in judicial processes and policy provisions. We have seen what can be done, which leads us to wonder: How much more of God's righteous reign could be embodied in our community and in our world were our churches to become more actively engaged in this mission? We suspect that our imagination is too limited.

Herein lies our disappointment. Despite what obviously can be done and what could be done by organizing bodies, why aren't more churches (particularly the dominant, white, evangelical, or mainline churches) working toward this incredibly attainable vision? Dan and I continue to expect the church to incarnate, not just discuss, what it is called to be. We recognize that we will not achieve full perfection, but we also yearn to see congregations embrace their potential. When we reflect on our calls to ministry, a common script quickly emerges. We look for a church that is so strange, so counter-culturally inclusive, so counter-intuitively free of fear and concern of self-preservation, so unique in vision that it can, in partnership with many allies, establish a beloved community in this world that reflects the jubilee of Israel that Mary hailed at hearing news of her conception, and that Jesus declared at his coming.

Sadly, despite the many victories described above, we see churches with this appetite and sustained practice only rarely. We see many, many churches obsessed with growth—though few of them succeed in this endeavor. Even the congregations most ardently devoted to reaching the unchurched generally succeed only in siphoning off members from other churches in the zero-sum Darwinian game of

American "church growth." "Beggar thy neighbor" practices drive increasing competition and aggressive marketing campaigns for the same population. Those on the losing side of this contest focus on survival, training all their resources on keeping the doors open, and hoping against hope that the next clergy will magically bring the young people back. Other congregations eschew the grow-or-perish marketing arena for the pursuit of right doctrine despite the glaring reality that their finely honed systematic theologies inevitably differ from folks down the street also honing theirs. This subtle competition of the mind, in our experience, often loses touch with the very fruit the church should bear, tending to produce not much more than animosity and isolationism.

Deep inside us is the gnawing lament that none of the above really sounds like the transformative gospel preached and embodied by Jesus. We don't fault our colleagues caught in the hamster wheels of working from week to week without sight of larger opportunities. We're naming sins we have committed. This is a systemic, collective problem—the commodified, competitive congregation does not look much like the church. In its long journey, Christianity has grown from a small, marginalized group to cultural hegemony in the West. Struggle has given way to entitlement; minority existence has been replaced by a sense of total control, even as this position of primacy is now being challenged. The vision and hope of Christianity that we call "the gospel" has been domesticated from the proud-scattering, throne-crushing vision of Mary in Luke 1:46–55, to a personal faith that so often reinforces our individual wants and fears while also reinforcing the divisions of class and social mobility. This evolution from public revolutionary faith to private cultural religion has been well chronicled by theologians and ecclesiologists.[4] Our focus in this book will be to point to a way of renewal, reinvigoration, and expanded engagement for the church by looking to the tools of community organizing to see just what might be. In doing so, we want to suggest what we all already know: the gospel is much larger and more comprehensive, more powerful and mobilizing, than the container we have made for it. While personal and spiritual, it is also material, social, political, and, yes, both local and global.

It is sad to say that so many congregations, for a variety of reasons, have missed, feared, or been unable to mobilize around the gospel that inspired Mary's Magnificat or Jesus' declaration of the jubilee in his first public teaching in Luke 4. In corroboration of this disappointment, Rev. Dr. William Barber, the President of North Carolina's NAACP and the convening leader of the Moral Movement in North Carolina, often proclaims that less than 10 percent of black churches were working actively with the Rev. Dr. Martin Luther King Jr. at Selma and in the movement he led.[5] From our observation, a similar marked absence of churches, conservative and liberal, currently characterizes the work of justice. The usual replies from the leaders of these congregations is that organizing is too confrontational, too time-intensive, too divisive, or simply a tangent to the true work of the gospel. We believe this is a tragedy on multiple counts. First and most importantly, this posture seems to miss the essence of Jesus' gospel. That is an assertion we'll defend readily in this book. Second, the work of organizing has not only the capability to empower churches to initiate and support meaningful social change in the world but also the powerful potential of transforming and reanimating congregations by aligning them with the sociopolitical rhythms and patterns of the gospel.

The purpose of this book is encapsulated in two strong images. The first speaks to the lament and the hope we have been describing.

Recently, a group of clergy from our local organizing affiliate traveled to East Baltimore as guests of Baltimoreans United in Leadership Development (BUILD), an older and more storied sister organization in the same national network.[6] In our meeting with these pastors and community organizers, we certainly witnessed the strong contrast between the city's opulent inner harbor and the visible scars of the recent Freddie Gray protests in several blighted communities—communities whose decades of tragic struggles were powerfully represented in HBO's series *The Wire*. The economic disparity and vacant homes were grim reminders of an unfinished task. But these were expected sights. What astounded us to tears was seeing row upon row of beautiful, affordable homes in East Baltimore. Standing on one particular street corner, we were unable to see a single apartment or row home that had not been recently renovated by BUILD and its partners, or a single vacant building that was not already owned by them and being prepared for restoration.

In alignment with the previous comments of Rev. Dr. Barber about the paucity of black church support for Rev. Dr. King, this revitalization had been accomplished, not by hundreds of congregations and faith-based communities, but by a handful. At one point, our clergy group asked our hosts about a specific church in the midst of this development. This local church was literally surrounded on every side by these sparkling new affordable homes. The change was all one could see from the church. We asked if that fellowship had been involved. "No," was their quick answer. They had politely declined invitations to join the work. Of course, we have no knowledge of the particular challenges or dreams of that church. For all we know, they could exceed the vision of kingdom around them in their own work. However, I (Tim) have struggled to come up with a proper analogy for their lack of involvement. It would be akin to standing in the middle of a beautiful 360-degree mural being painted, one that would change your daily vision forever, and never lifting a paintbrush or offering to brace a scaffold. On that street corner, we saw clear evidence of the immense potential and power of churches and faith-based communities to live into Jesus' kingdom. And yet, we also saw the source of the disappointment that frames the lament of this chapter. With such amazing possibility at hand, so few seem to find their way into this work. So many struggle to perceive the opportunities, or fear the inevitable realities of this labor.

The second image arises from the first time I toured the building our community rents for its weekly worship gatherings. During the tour, I learned the facility was the seventy-year-old property of a failing downtown church on its last breath. My guide that day was the congregation's last pastor. He had labored faithfully and passionately for five years, but was unable to stem the tide of an aging demographic as well as an entrenched and insulated traditionalism among the waning congregants. As our visit neared its end, the pastor took us out the rarely used front door; the church services for several months had been held in a small community room rather than the sanctuary. The front stoop, filled with leaves that marked its disuse, still offered a beautiful view of our rapidly growing city—an aging high school property turned into a thriving arts magnet public school, with its diverse student population eating lunch on the grounds right across the street; the once-vacant Duke family tobacco warehouses being revitalized as upscale lofts and trendy boutiques clearly visible in two directions; and a small skyline changing annually with new hotels and restaurants in the distance beyond the school and lofts. As our host took in the view, visible tears began running down his cheeks. "There is so much work to be done here. We could have mattered so much to this town." I just stood there in respectful silence, an onlooker to a lament addressed to an unseen congregation.

The image fits that disengaged congregation in East Baltimore as well. This book is an invitation to and a methodology for congregations to participate in vital missional labor, but the magnitude of that opportunity can be easily missed. The demise of that failed Durham church, from the hardly used front stoop to the dwindled congregation, is a tangible reminder that the external practices of mission are deeply enmeshed with the internal processes of community life. Mission and external kingdom work, or the lack thereof, are highly connected to expressions of this work inside communities.

In this text, we will offer seasoned and refined practices we have learned in the IAF (Industrial Areas Foundation), the NAACP, and other organizing communities, and apply the principles to the daily life of churches. This connection between external action and the daily, even mundane, lives of fellowships should not be surprising. Congregations, maybe *especially* congregations, are political spaces. They are intersections where power is gathered, invoked, and expressed. This is a truism for all communities, but uniquely true for churches, given the political nature of the gospel of Jesus. Intentionality in embodying this reality is the focus of community organizing. When this intentionality (and experience) is applied to congregations and is informed by a thick theological understanding of the church, congregations can be reanimated or thrive at unimagined levels of involvement. We invite pastors, congregational leaders, and the spiritually engaged to fully embrace this possibility. What we offer is not a technique or a congregational model, though we will discuss very specific practices. Instead, this is, at the foremost, a pattern for how to engage with one another shaped by the richness and political depth of the gospel. We have often wondered why so few congregations and faith communities unwittingly or intentionally fail to engage in substantive social change based on the stringent but hopeful demands of the gospel. But, as previously asserted, this book is about voluminous hope. We believe that the church has the great strength to impact the tone, logic, and politic of the world with the beautiful, gracious aspirations of Jesus' gospel.

At the heart of this book, then, is a vision of the church that takes concrete form in the renewal and activation of congregations. A vibrant community will function like any breathing organism, embracing a cycle of inward and outward movement: inhaling and exhaling. The practices of organizing, we believe, offer a crucial way of both faithfully revitalizing our congregations and then mobilizing them for mission.[7] The former is something that all too often organizers and scholars writing on organizing have failed to realize. We suspect they tend to overlook because they avoid a theological interrogation of organizing–what we hope to be our unique contribution. Viewing ourselves as organic theologians who work within the questions and concerns raised by pastors and churches trying to discern if organizing is something they should embrace, we want to address concerns about "How does this fit with the teaching of the gospel and work the church is called to do?" Also, "How will my congregation benefit from and see its faith enriched by organizing practices?"

While the academic study of community organizing is starting to grow, rarely do scholars engage these kinds of questions, as they tend to prefer socioscientific explanation rather than theological interpretation. This can appear as an attempt to justify the practice, which often fails to be convincing to church leaders and members, and also doesn't inspire them to engage in the work. Most congregations are not primarily interested in the future of democracy or the state of civil society, but in the future of their congregations. A "theology of organizing" therefore feels essential, something pastors engaged in the work already sense is needed, but requires further discussion.

Second, mobilization speaks to those ministers and leaders seeking to find ways to "get their congregations in the game" of serious and sustained social change. Many churches are poised with a vision of social liberation rooted in the gospel of Jesus and resourced to support the ongoing work of structural social justice. And many of these same fellowships are deeply disappointed, unable to translate this generative vision into practice. The practices and commitments we detail in this book are significant steps toward the actualization of those often frustrated hopes. We have seen this transformation from intent to meaningful action in the church we led together for ten years. We have also witnessed it in other churches and faith communities deploying these practices–many quite different in theology, tradition, and organization from the church we pastored.

There is a wonderful way forward for leaders and ministers in revitalizing and empowering churches, but to reiterate, this book is not a strict program or even a manual. It is not a model or a prefabricated set of steps. Instead, it is a field guide for pastors and church leaders desiring to build healthy congregations, deepen the culture of discipleship, and respond to the adaptive challenges of the twenty-first century. It is a skill set, or, better, as our friend Rev. Jim Honig has put it, offers "a constellation of artful practices" for activating a congregation that will necessarily require the skills of improvisation, adjustment, and curtailing in your context. While we have certainly written it so the chapters can be read sequentially, and early chapters will inform those that follow, we also hope you will return to specific chapters at various points as you work to enrich and embolden your community. Your church will not look like ours. And that is as it should be.

Finally, we've intentionally tried to make this text useful to diverse faith communities—both inside and outside the Christian tradition—even as our account is indelibly shaped by the gospel of Jesus Christ.[8] Our next chapter intentionally explores the identity and theology of the Christian church and its distinct calling to and potential for organizing in the cause of justice according to the vision of Jesus' kingdom. But for those outside the Christian tradition, feel free to move to our third chapter on power. We invite you to read our whole text through the lens of your own tradition, commitments, and worldview, in a shared pursuit of justice and peace. Our experience in organizing has always been religiously ecumenical and has engaged ethical traditions or worldviews outside of formal religions. We are deeply confident that the practices we describe in this book will be transformative and meaningful across this whole spectrum. As co-laborers and fellow pilgrims, we invite you to glean from what we offer, make use of what you find helpful, begin where you discern is best, and refract it through your own style and context, that the peculiarity of deep community and justice-oriented ministry work might be manifest in your particular congregation or community.

2

RE-DEFINING the Church: Practice-Based Ecclesiology

There is much discussion about the future of the church in the U.S. While we tend to be more optimistic than pessimistic (depending on the daily news), our hopes for the church are challenged by some deep frustrations. We often find ourselves wishing we did not have to admit what the famed sociologist Peter Berger has said: "Both those who have great hopes for the role of religion in the affairs of this world and those who *fear* this role must be disappointed by the factual evidence."[1] True, religious belief and the church have not been as violent or destructive as those who want to see them abolished from the public sphere charge. But for us, it is the first part of his statement that continually leaves us troubled. And it is why, while we recognize the many wounds the church has inflicted, we still see immeasurable possibilities for the body.

As we begin, it is worth stepping back a bit to consider the social body we are talking about. We need to address some basic questions: *What* is the church? *Where* is it? and *Why* church? (or, What's its true purpose?) Our discussion of the church here, or what in theological terms would be called ecclesiology, will not be exhaustive, but is meant to invite the reader who longs to see the church revived to consider more closely the peculiar nature of this unique community. For lay leaders and clergy yearning for renewal in the church, some expansive discussion is well worth the effort. Clarity regarding the identity and essential actions of the church is critical for engaging in a discussion about future possibilities.

We also want to offer one caveat up front. The church we describe will include some obvious components, but, as is the aim of this book, we will also contend that there are certain practices of the church that need to be rehabilitated or recovered if the community is to be reanimated and renewed. While some terms, such as the "recognition of gifts," the "open meeting," and the "rule of Christ" may be unfamiliar to you, retrieving these early church practices is indeed essential for congregational revitalization and activation. These ecclesial practices both infuse and ground the work of community organizing, helping to provide a theological framework for the practices we will discuss throughout the book.

What Is the Church?

At the beginning of his discussion of creation in the *Confessions,* Augustine of Hippo contemplates the enigmatic notion of time. In doing so, he relates that on the one hand, he seems to understand time rather easily as a term or concept used in everyday conversation. And yet, on the other hand, he notes, whenever he begins to consider the notion closely, it eludes and confuses him. Similarly, we often have the same experience when thinking about or discussing "the church." On the one hand, it's a term we use routinely without much difficulty or confusion. No one seems confounded when I (Dan) tell them that on Christmas Eve I went to church, or if I were to say that I serve on our church's finance committee (though, of course, no wise congregation would let me do this). On the other hand, we find that when we try to describe more specifically what we mean by the term "church," we quickly begin to stumble over our words only to offer some muddled, usually long-winded and significantly qualified, definition. For we persons deeply involved with the church, it seems so familiar, and yet, when pressed, we recognize that it remains also rather foreign.

Back in Sunday school, we learned fairly early on that the church is not a building and that it is distinct from other organizations such as the city council, the country club, or IBM. Instead, we remember, we were taught that it is the people gathered together as disciples of Jesus in the worship of God. While this is a good beginning, we recognize that it is also still rather vague. Is singing a hymn with friends by the campfire considered "church"? Is simply watching or going through the motions of a rite of liturgy "church"? Is praying with a group of believers in the morning before school or listening to a sermon on the radio "church"? Maybe in part, but not exactly.

Looking to scripture as a way of beginning to gain a clearer definition of the church is appropriate. "Church" (*ecclesia*), however, is not a term frequently used in the Bible. As a word borrowed from Greco-Roman culture, it carries the meaning of an assembly gathered to do political work, to make decisions, or to deliberate on issues, even as we recognize that its definition is uniquely expanded in scripture. Most significantly, as Matthew 18:20 tells us, this public assembly is one gathered in the presence of Christ, an assembly where Jesus is present. Christ's presence in the assembly is not to be viewed here as some kind of disembodied idea or internal feeling. It is the real presence of Jesus Christ through the Spirit incarnate in the *community* as it partakes in the love and forgiveness that characterizes Jesus' way. Joined to the person of the risen Christ by the Spirit, the church is the gathered community united to the life of the triune God. Its life of discipleship together embodies a new people, a social body whose relations and practices manifest, even if imperfectly, human communion with God. It is this reality that allows Paul in 1 Corinthians 12 and Romans 12 to describe the church as Christ's body.

No mere human creation, the church is a work of God. It is a creature of the good news manifest and active in Jesus Christ, the first fruits of a new creation restored to communion with the God whose very life is love. Its own communal existence is made possible and structured by the communal life of the triune God.[2] A foretaste of the fully consummated kingdom, the church is those people gathered as the embodiment of the reign of God, whose very love, grace, righteousness, and forgiveness define and shape their community. While certainly not perfect, it is the social body in which humanity is uniquely restored in our relation to God and thereby in whom the new relations of the kingdom are made available. Within the corpus of the New Testament, therefore, the assembly is consistently defined as a new "people," a "holy nation," a "royal priesthood" (1 Pet. 2:9), a "new humanity," the "household of God" (Eph. 2:15, 19; Heb. 3:6; 1 Tim. 3:15), or a "commonwealth" of heaven (Phil. 3:20). The reality of the church that emerges from scripture is a social body whose very activity, organization, life, and relations are restored to unity with the essentially relational God.

One danger in writing a book on church reanimation—and especially one on organizing practices within the church—is inadvertently to construe the church as merely human in nature. That the church is essentially dependent upon the gift of Christ's presence cannot be stressed enough. Yet, at the same time, it is a tangible, human community no less real than the U.S. Marines, the University of Alabama, the nation of Brazil, or, heaven help us, our own extended families. As a real creation of the living God we encounter in Jesus and made known in scripture, the church is a social body whose existence is historical, material, and political. As with any human community, its organization takes a regular and rather stable form in historically accepted ways of doing things or interacting with one another that give shape to it as a social body. A distinctive pattern of life based on the path carved by the person and teaching of Jesus arises in connection with an observable and divinely instituted set of social practices (sacraments) that define the community, an order and pattern present in each local community but also shared universally even if not exactly replicated in each gathering. It goes without saying that the church is not a static community, however. As a real living community, it is shaped by the tradition of these practices, but they also must be practiced anew with each generation and in each particular gathering—for God is not the God of the dead but of the living (Mk. 12:27; Mt. 22:32; Lk. 20:38). The church is thus the genuine (though imperfect and incomplete) presence in human history of a people who in their communion together are being narrated into the life of the living God.[3] A divine institution, it is also a fully human, social reality tangibly present in the local congregation and united universally in its origin and end.

While we have clarified to some extent what the church is, our answer to the question has only led us to ask another one, namely: *Where* is this church? How do you know it when you see it? or, Where can you point to this church? In order to more fully answer *what* the church is, we realize we must attempt to designate *where* it is. To this we now turn.

Where Is the Church?

We are certainly not the first to entertain the question of trying to determine what designates the presence of the church. As with the question "What is the church?" this one, too, has perplexed generations of theologians, Protestant and Catholic. In an attempt to locate the church, Martin Luther identified seven essential marks. John Calvin famously proclaimed that the church existed wherever the Word was rightly preached and the sacraments properly administered. Catholics have argued that the church is most fully present in the celebration of the Eucharist, where the bishop represents the unified people. The sketch we offer below is based in practice, or in what churches do and how they do what they do. It is widely ecumenical, relying quite heavily on what we have learned from other Christian communions, but it also has a baptist (small "b") or free-church tilt.[4] As will become obvious, this is not because we privilege individual autonomy and spirituality or because we fear institutions. Instead, what we hope to show is that critical to the renewal and revitalization of the church in our age is the true practice of a community politic that recognizes the gifts of each member, engages in open and vulnerable dialogue allowing every voice to speak, attends graciously to the wrongs and conflicts that occur in the community and plague the world, and continuously participates in the corporate practice of interpreting and discerning what it means to be disciples of Jesus in the current context. When a privileged clericalism doesn't crowd out others' gifts and when communal discernment accompanies the practice of baptism, the study of scripture, solidarity with the poor, and the celebration of communion, a thicker community of disciples committed to the mission and way of Jesus appears.

As discussed above, the church is the people of God gathered in the presence of Christ to do God's business by the power of the Holy Spirit. But this should not be mistaken for just any other assembly. The church is not a rock concert, a town-hall meeting, or a running club, even as it may bear some semblance of these. One of the central things the past generation of postliberal theologians has taught us is that the church, insofar as the first communities understood it, is a distinct people. What they meant by this is that the Christian community is a peculiar way of life. It inhabits its own particular narrative begun in Israel, made known in scripture, and centered on Jesus' life, death, and resurrection. This story shapes its own ethic, making the community a peculiar people with their own pattern of relations, mutual expectations, and shared vision and mission. To say that the church is an ethic implies that it is embodied in a cluster of specific practices—practices that form the normal habits of action for those in the community. Constituted in these practices, the church is a politic—that is, a corporate body whose life manifests the new humanity made possible in Jesus. In this way, the church in and through its practices embodies a true public alternative to the distorted and violent structures that govern the world (Eph. 2:2; Col. 2:20). Thus, the church is where those gathered under the Lordship of Jesus perform these distinct social practices. *There* is the church.

So what are these distinctive practices? In what follows, we offer a brief description of the *six practices* we take to be definitive for locating the church. While we offer a sketch of each of them, we don't mean to presume that they must be practiced exactly the same in each congregation, even as we do assert that they must at least be recognizable by way of their connection to the depiction of each in scripture. Additionally, the list is not meant to be exhaustive, sequential, or linear. Not everything churches do is included, nor are the practices conducted in some rigid order. Indeed, it is essential to the integrity of the practices themselves that they enfold, overlap, and mutually inform one another in a way that establishes a certain structuring rhythm.

I (Dan) recently read an article that reported the ill effects on health for those who work night shifts. Beyond the obvious toll this schedule would foreseeably take on one's quality of sleep, the study covered in the article found that the effects were even more troubling. Looking at data of nurses who worked the night shift, researchers found that those working this rotating schedule for five years or more had lower life-expectancy and were at increased-risk of dying of cardiovascular disease. Those who worked this schedule for fifteen years or more were more likely to die of lung cancer, adding an additional malady to earlier studies that had already linked this work schedule to brain and heart problems. What most intrigued me about the article, however, was that researchers determined the underlying issue to be the disruption of the body's circadian rhythm, or the endogenous biological clock native to humans and all living things.[5] It appears that there is a basic rhythm of activity constitutive of biological life, a rhythm that if continually disrupted can result in dire effects on the organism.

When we speak of the rhythm associated with this constellation of practices, we refer to something similar to the circadian rhythm of an organism. Here it's simply that we have in mind a social (or communal) rhythm. Just as with circadian rhythms, we contend that to the extent that some of the practices composing this rhythm are abandoned or not performed fully, the community itself becomes hobbled, distorted, and maybe even detrimental to itself. We've found, however, that the work of organizing has brought us back to some of these practices and helped us recover their importance for congregational vitality. Most congregations we've encountered do practice some version, however thin, of each of these practices, but organizing has helped us realize just how essential it is to intentionally attend to their collective rehabilitation.

Finally, all of these social practices should be understood as sacramental in nature, meaning that in them God acts in, under, over, and with the frailties of human action. Being sacramental does not mean they are magical. The community does not gain control of God by performing them. However, acting in faithful obedience to God's promise to show up in these corporate practices, the community can expect that God is present in Christ by the power of the Spirit when it does them.

*   *   *

The first practice of the constellation we want to highlight is that of *baptism.* Following in the example and instruction of Jesus, whose own baptism by John in the Jordan River exhibited his willing obedience to the Father (Mt. 3:13–17; Mk. 1:9–11; Lk. 3:21–22), and who then commissioned his disciples with the authority to carry it on (Mt. 28:14–15), the early church adopted this practice as a rite of initiation, marking visibly and tangibly the making of a new people. More than simply a kind of hazing meant to cultivate identification with and devotion to the group, passing through the waters of baptism is nothing less than participation in the death and resurrection of Jesus Christ. That is to say, it is entrance into an entirely new world, the new creation (2 Cor. 5:17). The cleansing waters usher one out of the power of sin and death and into a new life in a "new humanity" (Eph. 2:15). The gracious work of God, baptism brings one out of the old world of division, violence, and oppression under the principalities and powers ordered to death, and into the new people united in the living presence of Christ. In the gift of baptism, the old divisions of race, gender, and status are nullified and entrance is provided into a people of peace in whom the walls of hostility have been broken down (Gal. 3:28; Eph. 2:14). Thus, in the practice of baptism, all other allegiances—whether they be racial or national, tribal or familial, economic or political—are redefined and usurped by the freedom and independence of the new creation. Hence, the community is established anew in each generation through the act of initiating and integrating newly graced members. Baptism is not the erasure of differences but the joining of them in the formation of a new people, a people drawn from every tribe and tongue into the person and way of Jesus.

One's initiation into the new humanity does not culminate in passive membership. Instead, active participation in the community is divinely gifted to each member for the health and upbuilding of the people, with each person called to play a distinctly identifiable

and essential role in this encouragement. The second practice that
marks the presence of the church, therefore, is what we might call
the *recognition of gifts*. At a time when there is much anxiety and
handwringing over the future of the clergy and priesthood, when
there is much concern about the bureaucracy of the episcopacy in
various congregations, we think the real recovery of a decentralized,
deprofessionalized, less hierarchical, and lay-driven form of ministry
may be ripe for recovery. Such a mode of church order is more
resonant with the structure of early churches. Within the community,
the scriptural vision indicates that each and every member has been
divinely endowed with a specific gift essential to the very functioning
of the church as the body of Christ (1 Cor. 12:7; Eph. 4:16). In the
"fullness of Christ" (Eph. 4:13) there really is no "lay" member, if
by this we mean having no ministry. But as a part of Christ's saving
work and the perfection of God's reign, each has been assigned a gift
integral to the functioning of the whole (1 Cor. 7:7; Eph. 4:7–8; 1 Pet.
4:10).[6] These giftings should not be mistaken for natural or innate
talents, for they are peculiar gifts of the Spirit often given to the
most unassuming of members for the complete functioning of the
people. Neither should these giftings be misconstrued as assembly-
line style tasks, as if they were some version of modern economic
specialization of labor under the management of a visionary leader.
Instead, in the biblical perspective, all are ministers and given to lead
in certain areas in interdependence with one another.

There is no doubt that the community will recognize some to
bear the specific roles of instructors, of caring for the corporate
gathering, or of offering prophetic challenge. But at the same time,
they will acknowledge that these roles are part of a structure in
which each member has a divinely apportioned authority, equal
dignity, and mutual accountability. Functioning with respect to the
Spirit's distribution of gifts is more than democratic, for it is not
simply that each has a vote or is represented in the basic operations
of the community. Each member has something unique to offer
to the good of the community that, if left undone or dismissed,
significantly weakens the body. Because it eschews an emphasis on
central, dominant leaders and institutional officials, this mark of the
church is likely the one least practiced by our communities. As a
result, our churches often do not embody the full participation and
empowerment of gifts they could under the headship of Christ.

The third practice of the church is more familiar to most of us
than the recognition of gifts, even if there is some standing diversity
in the way we conduct it. The *table meal*, or Eucharist, or communion,

is common to all Christian communities. Indeed, at the heart of the Christian way of life and the center of the constellation of practices that determine that way of life is this community meal. Before his death, Jesus established this practice for his followers, instructing them to continue in its regular practice (Lk. 22:14–20). It was the focal point of the early church's gathering and was understood to be essential to the ongoing distinctive life of the community (Acts 2:42; 1 Cor. 11:23–26). Here, Jesus the Christ was really present to his followers in the bread and wine of the meal gathering. The *koinonia* of the table manifests and incarnates the community's unity with the crucified and risen Christ, and therefore with the triune life of God, and with one another, which is our true end. As the Greek Orthodox theologian John Zizioulas notes, it is our sharing in the communion of the table fellowship (the Eucharist) by which the church most realizes and incarnates its unity with the triune God, because its communion shares in the very communion that is the Trinity. In sharing the meal, the church embodies Christ (who is really present with and in them) in human history and its hope for the future without bringing that history to an end.[7] As a recurrent practice of the community, in the table we partake of and are made collective participants in the overflowing gracious love that is the triune life.

As we have mentioned, this meal is a radical act of communion, one that should manifest itself throughout the community in the loving interdependence of mutual service and provision. For John's gospel, this is displayed by the incorporation of the practice of "foot washing" that precedes the table fellowship (Jn. 13:1–17). Additionally, in many gatherings, the corporate praying of the Lord's Prayer serves as entry to the table, in request that God really make this act one that embodies the restored relations and mutual care of God's kingdom. Hence it is the Corinthians' failure to embody the full unity and provision of the table that has Paul so steamed in his communication with them (1 Cor. 11:17–34). Not simply a mystical rite performed for an audience of spectators, the table is a real economic act, the sharing of the basic necessities of life (bread and wine) in participation and celebration of God's abundant grace.[8] That is to say, it is a new ethic, configured not by competition, individualism, or scarcity and violence, but by the abundant and dynamic love of the living God. In short, the practice of the common table marks the church as it actively institutes the peaceful unity and restoration of the new humanity.

Following on the unity practiced at the table meal, the fourth defining mark of the church comes into view: *solidarity with the poor and marginalized.* It is a clear distinctive of the biblical church that it takes a particular interest in and maintains a close connection with the disinherited of this world. It may somewhat offend our American industrial sensibilities, but Jesus' career was one of homelessness, marginalization, and poverty (Mt. 8:20; Mk. 6:2–6). His teaching privileged the poor, even going so far as to announce their liberation, and he taught his disciples to see his presence in those wedged under the heels of society and in need (Lk. 4:18–21; Mt. 25:31–46). Over and over again, we see the disinherited, the sick, the troubled, and the destitute flocking to Jesus. Clearly, one of the distinctive aspects of the early community of his followers depicted in Acts was their solidarity with one another, and especially with those on the underside of society—a mixing of social stratifications and disregard for etiquette that often got them into trouble. While the church certainly included persons from all segments of society, part of its uniqueness was its close association with the poor, marginalized, and disinherited.

San Salvador's Archbishop Oscar Romero spoke to a gathering at the University of Louvain, Belgium, in February of 1980, just a month before he would be assassinated by government soldiers for preaching against their reign of violence. He described the church's association with the poor as its "true home," commenting that its renewed encounter with the poor has effected a "conversion" within the church to the "central truth of the gospel." He continued, "In a word, the church has not only turned toward the poor, it has made of the poor the special beneficiaries of its mission because, as Puebla says, 'God takes on their defense and loves them.'"[9] Romero was not promoting here a gospel of health and wealth, a message of personal advance or individual blessing more akin to the heterodox "American dream" than the good news of Jesus. Instead, he was drawing off of Catholic Social Thought to point beyond mere generosity and toward the cultivation of real community. Envisioned here is a new kind of society—forged in gathering with those shunned, rejected, and oppressed by the powers that order and rule a fallen world, distinctively marking the church in its liberation from and resistance to those structures (Col. 2:15; Eph. 6:12).

The Catholic womanist scholar M. Shawn Copeland states:

> A Christian praxis of solidarity denotes the
> humble and complete orientation of ourselves
> before the lynched Jesus, whose shadow falls

across the table of our sacramental meal. In his
raised body, a compassionate God interrupts
the structures of death and sin, of violation and
oppression. A divine praxis of solidarity sets
the dynamics of love against the dynamics of
domination–recreating and regenerating the
world, offering us a new way of being in relation
to God, to others, to self.[10]

The result is, in fact, a new structure, a new power of the church that
moves *with* the vulnerable, poor, and marginalized to enact together
a new freedom. Such solidarity is one of the marks the twenty-first-
century church, all across its denominational spectrum, is in dire
need of recovering. A church without the poor and marginalized is
no church at all.

Of course, learning to live in freedom requires training and
continual education in the way of Jesus through faithful engagement
with and communal study of the scripture (Jn. 5:39; Acts 17:11).
Hence, the fifth mark of the church is the recurrent practice of
scriptural study and formation. Such a practice could most certainly
include the exercise of preaching and the public reading of
scripture, but it should also incorporate the participation of the
entire community in the prayerful interpretation and application
of biblical teaching. We have written extensively elsewhere on this
theme, so we need not rehash our arguments here.[11] But suffice it
to say that discipleship in the way of Jesus is a communal effort,
one conducted as an ongoing exercise of collective hermeneutics
of the texts esteemed to be authoritative witnesses to his life and
way. Echoing the affirmation of our friends in their statement on
"Re-envisioning Baptist Identity," a process of scriptural deliberation
marks the church that offers voice to everyone, silencing no one, so
that the full content of the gospel might be recognized, received,
and embraced.[12] Certainly, such a practice is mirrored in the actions
of Catholic base communities or Wesleyan class meetings, and may
have some semblance to the widespread implementation of small
groups or the origination of house churches though with a more
intentional commitment to diversity. Encountering again and again
the good news of God's kingdom and allowing this message to shape
our lives are constitutive of the church.

The last indicative practice of the church, and the one we are
most earnest to stress for the purposes of this book, is that of the *rule
of Christ* or what might otherwise be called the *politics of forgiveness.*

or the practice of *binding and loosing*. Indeed, we suggest that the recovery of this practice within our ecclesial communities is really the key to their renewal and revitalization. But we recognize that at this point, it may not be clear what we are referring to when we speak of the rule of Christ. Established most fully by Jesus in Matthew 18:15–20, wherein he instructs the "church" on how to deal with offenses committed against one another, the rule of Christ is a social process of accountability (binding) and forgiveness (loosing) aimed at reconciliation.[13] It's an ecclesial procedure for engaging fractures, disputes, and wrongs within the community as a way of seeking to reestablish solidarity between opponents and to reconstitute the *koinonia* of its society.

Like any other human community, the church suffers divisions. Given the great value that so many place on their faith and its hopes, the wounds that result from the inevitable fractures and conflicts are great and seemingly permanent. We have all been there, as victims and perpetrators of division! An absence of reconciliation threatens every aspect of the identity of the church and its mission. Thus, critical to its endurance in faithfulness is the practice of what theologian James McClendon has called a "politics of forgiveness," allowing the church to resolve conflicts and make decisions in harmony. Defined as "a never-ending congregational *conversation* about Jesus' way—a conversation that may now engage only two or three, but again will involve the gathered ἐκκλησία itself," the rule of Christ is a mode of participatory governance necessary for sustaining the identity of the community.[14] Though beginning at a personal level and in connection to a tangible, local issue, it might involve the counsel and help of the entire congregation for resolving the disagreement and restoring unity. Bearing responsibility for one another, this participatory mode of deliberation is not punitive in nature, but seeks in open vulnerability to admonish faithfulness through forgiveness, seeking what might be learned from the situation. Intimately intertwining the practice of responsible forgiveness with the process of collective discernment, this practice offers the entire community the chance to speak into and provide insight on the issue and situation as is consistent with the Spirit-filled deliberation scripture depicts as being characteristic of the church (Acts 15; 1 Cor. 14).[15]

While we may not countenance every element of her process theology, we affirm the insights theologian Catherine Keller draws from Martin Luther King Jr.'s *Letter from Birmingham Jail* concerning the interrelatedness of life to emphasize the nature of relationality and forgiveness as "becoming." For her, the sustained work of forgiveness and mutuality "deepens who I am, who I am becoming, amidst my living relations. And what I become influences what you may become."[16] She offers a strong descriptive addendum to McClendon's explanation of the discerning politics of forgiveness. As she describes, this is a persistent work of relationship that drives love we may hold for each other toward embodied justice, letting "passion grow into the justice of com/passion," so as to remind us that the passion of forgiveness enacted in justice is always a "passion-with the other." [17] This, of course, takes time, requires openness to correction and adjustment, and necessitates the hard work of listening and vulnerably trying to understand one another.

Combining in this process both a relational procedure for working things out between one another and collective decision-making, the rule of Christ is the ongoing practice of an open conversation that seeks resolution and wisdom through unforced consensus as a mode of governance capable of putting the community back on track or allowing it to know how to move forward when the way is unclear.

In contrast to the fragmentation of individual autonomy, the oppressiveness of dictatorship, the vagaries of majority rule, or the centralization of clerical management, the rule of Christ is thus a unique style of community formation (reformation and reconstitution) wherein the community is harmonized to make authoritative judgments (Mt. 18:19–20). As such it is rule-bound without succumbing to legalism; it is creative and flexible without devolving into chaos or relativism. Incorporating fraternal admonition, deliberation, and practical discernment, it allows the community to address wrongs, attend to new circumstances, learn new information, and modify hurtful or divisive structures.[18] Thus, this process for decision-making provides a way for the community to remain true to its tradition without becoming stuck in immutable prescriptions—for example, allowing it to come to honor previously suppressed giftings (for instance, as with the ordination of women), and to reassess and realign its own practices (as when the practice of the table goes awry, as it did in Corinth). *It is in this practice that the church discovers the power and leading of the Spirit for building strong and healthy relationships, enacting the full scope of its mission, and obtaining wisdom for how faithfully to remain on track and to move forward. Through this practice of the rule of Christ, the community determines what it means to live here and now within the freedom of Christ's victory and under the gracious reign of God.*

* * *

It may seem we have described a church that exists nowhere. No church we've led or visited performs these six practices perfectly. And yet, if we view them charitably, we think many of the vestiges or outlines of these practices can be seen in a wide array of communities and their ecclesial structures. Granted, current practices may be distorted in many ways, and some of them are not being performed fully. Nonetheless, a powerfully distinct way of life still arises in connection to these mundane practices, even if its power is not fully realized and its resources not fully tapped. As we mentioned above, one of the inspirations for us in writing this book was the conviction that a recovery of the final practice of the rule of Christ, while relying on the others, is essential to the restoration and renewal of our congregations. It is also, we think, essential to the work of organizing and, oddly enough, one we were brought back to as a result of our engagement in the work of community organizing. Hence, we suggest the core of the crisis our congregations face is the result of a failure to practice collective discernment and corporate governance such that a recovery of this key practice is essential to reinvigorating the internal and missional life of our communities. Later in the book, we will even go so far as to contend that conflict, when addressed faithfully, is necessary and helpful within the life of the community, illustrating how the rule of Christ in application can provide an essential function within the mobilization of our communities.

Why the Church? (Or, Whither the Church?)

All of this discussion of the church—*what* it is, and *where* it is—makes little difference if we do not have a sense of *why* the church exists and where it is headed. As with everything else, its end determines its meaning and significance. So, finally, in our discussion of the church, we want to sketch the *why* and *whither* of this social body as a way of providing a trajectory for the kind of constructive work we want to privilege. If, as Ephesians 4:12–16 communicates, the work of ministry is intimately connected to "building up the body of Christ," then we realize that we are all called to participate in the work of this construction, joining in unity and maturity as a unique whole body whose ongoing upbuilding and growth in love constitutes its mission. Again, the discussion above on where the church can be found has led us to inquire about this community's purpose or reason for existing.

Alfred Loisy's sardonic comment that "Jesus announced the Kingdom, but it was the church that came," as theologian Robert Jenson has noted, is not altogether just a joke. Still, the reality of the church is initiated by the fact that God does not will for the resurrection to be the end. Instead, Jesus' victorious work is extended through the delaying of the parousia, making time for the church to play a role in its unfolding.[19] Thus, the church is the creature of this decisive and protracted event. It exists for the purpose of embodying and making known the good news of God's saving, liberating, and healing work because, as Stanley Hauerwas has been so keen to reiterate, the church does not *have* an ethic but it *is* an ethic; the church is also the mission.[20] What we mean to say by this is that the church exists to gather humanity in the community of God's people as the vehicle in and through which God's renewing of creation is made visibly present. The church is called to be now what the world restored to God's reign will be in the future. Its end is the fully consummated and embodied kingdom.

From the perspective of its end, the church is first called to bear witness to this future. As the first fruits of new creation, it is to be a tangible foretaste, beachhead, or colony of a creation restored to communion with God. That is to say, its corporate practices provide alternative structures powerful in their own right for cultivating and sustaining a new humanity. This does not mean that its communal life will always be perfect and that it will never falter, lapse into division, or experience conflict, but that its very distinctiveness may be most on display in the way it engages in these situations to seek forgiveness, foster reconciliation, adjust structures where needed, and faithfully discern a way forward when the path is not clear. Attesting in its own internal organization to the love and peace that have victoriously triumphed in Jesus Christ, the church exists to embody this new reality, a people innovatively exhibiting this new possibility within a distorted society as what Martin Luther King Jr. once called "the creatively maladjusted."[21] United with Jesus Christ, whose presence in the Spirit shapes and enlivens the community, the church becomes a tangible experimental society for an ever more creative means of building unity and seeking peace as it grows in the triune life of abundant love.

The practices that structure the new life made available in this alternative community also form a base from which to engage the needs and issues that plague a world still lost to sin and death. Those who have learned the art of forgiving governance aimed at communion, attentiveness to the least of these, reliance upon the diversity of gifts, and collective discernment with the community of the church, James McClendon suggests, will not find it hard to adapt these practices to contexts outside the community as a service of pursuing peace, justice, and healing in mission to the world.[22] In this way the church, following its Lord, gives itself for the world.

Much has been made about the new context of post-Christendom in which the church now exists. Of course, it impacts each congregation differently. Some see it as a threat to their legacy, as they attempt to deal with a fledgling congregation in an era of disestablishment. Others see this as a profound opportunity for renewed service and mission. One of these latter voices has been Stuart Murray, whose view of the post-Christendom church envisions an exciting, new era for mission. As Murray recognizes, by accepting its marginal status, the church can actually engage in a freer kind of service as a result of not having to be in control. Describing the power of powerlessness, he states, "Powerless churches need not wrangle over the relationship between evangelism and social action (this was always essentially about power), but can develop fresh perspectives on seemingly intractable social issues, because things look different from the margins."[23] Free to enact a peculiar kind of service, the church can interface with the powers, structures, and orders of the world to seek new positive and creative alternatives—as it is not bound by the same strictures of efficiency, retribution, management, or safety. Instead, it can take risks and pilot new approaches for addressing issues. As Larry Rasmussen puts it, the community of the church will engage in "creative deviance on the front line"—deviant because it does not accept the norms of culture, creative because it offers a positive alternative.[24]

Aimed toward a unique end, the church moves in witness and service to the world as a community freed from the need to be in control, allowing it to be uniquely creative in its mission of expanding and cultivating the kingdom. Its fidelity to Christ and the gift of his presence allow it to embody a real alternative. And its hope for the full consummation of this end allows it to move as a pioneering people who seek to see Christ's healing and renewal become actualized across the whole of creation.

*   *   *

In many ways, the church does not seem peculiar, for, as you likely know, it often fails to live into its calling or to embody its potential. Yet, at times, it really does act as the body of Christ. We presume that, like us, seeing these flashes are what's kept you around. This church, with all its faults, persists as a peculiar people, a community gathered despite itself, sometimes, in a pioneering hope. It is just this peculiar living hope we so want to see become invigorated and expanded through the renewal and revitalization of some of the very basic practices of our community. And we think that the tools of community organizing offer a resource for doing just this. As we will go on to show, there can be a natural connection between the artful practices of community organizing and congregational regeneration that is not theologically naïve or dismissive. If organizing is cultivated and developed, we believe it can help us more fully recover some of the marks described above, and catalyze rehabilitated congregations to tangibly care for the larger community they inhabit. Organizing can help the church recover what it means to embody Christ and to manifest more fully the hope his presence in our world provides.

3

RE-EMPOWERING the Church: Why Power Matters for Congregations

"Power" in church contexts is usually a dirty word. It smacks of everything the church should not be: violent, competitive, duplicitous, and opportunist. It's no accident that good church folk bristle when the theme comes up and seek to expel it from the workings of the congregation. Power, in our society, is Machiavellian, the intrinsically corrupt but necessary tool of politicians and military generals in a complicated and fallen world—something that can at best be balanced in order for some semblance of peace to occur. Surely if Lord Acton was right, that "power corrupts and absolute power corrupts absolutely," then there's good reason to try to keep it out of the church. I think we all can attest to the disaster of a church given over to an ends-justifies-the-means political climate.

Yet, as is all too obvious, there's no way out of power, and when we're not playing coy, we think ministers and leaders must admit that power is necessary. In all honesty, those of us who have it *like* having it, and those of us who lack it either wish we had it and are trying to get it, or have simply given up. In our experience, it's often those who have quite a bit of power who tend not to want to talk about it or recognize it within the purified confines of the church. This is especially the case for upper middle-class white folks, who tend to enjoy the benefit of power more generally. Often what scares us about power is first and foremost the fact that, should we begin to recognize it, then we'd have to begin to recognize how much of it we have relative to others. Recognizing power means recognizing how frequently we get our way and how the existing structures benefit us more than others.

It's usually at this point that the fear of power arises in the context of community organizing. As the flip side of privilege, we fear, organizing power appears as insurgent power, a forceful uprising of those on the bottom in an attempt to claim that privileged place for themselves. Indeed, this apprehension about the role of power in organizing is not completely unfounded. Saul Alinsky, the brilliant if acerbic mid-twentieth century pioneer of community organizing, has said that if Machiavelli's *The Prince* was a treatise for the powerful on how to hold on to their power, then organizing is a practice of how to empower those who are not powerful.[1] There's no doubt that too often this can feel as if it's just shifting the same old field of play simply to the other side. In this chapter, we offer a theological engagement with the theme of power to argue that, while Alinsky's view of power needs to be refined within the life of the people of God, there is much to learn from community organizing about how to build healthy power in our communities. We want to suggest that power, while maybe a bit tricky to navigate, is essential to the life of a vibrant and active congregation. Indeed, we will even go so far as to say that a peculiar practice of building and organizing power is intrinsic to the church as a community born of the gospel of Jesus Christ. For it is a peculiar kind of power that gives shape to the church itself, making it what it is and allowing it to move in reconciliation, peace, and justice to fulfill its mission.

Defining Power

What is power? This may seem like a straightforward question, but it's something worth clarifying at this point. I (Dan) teach in the social justice program at Loyola University Chicago's Institute of Pastoral Studies, where I get to engage with an amazing group of energetic and wonderfully agitated students around the issues and problems that plague our society. Power is something, I've found, that my students both understand and yet need to learn. They are typically well acquainted with power as coercion, and usually coercion in its crudest forms—whether these be violent actions or the microaggressions of language or prejudice. This oversimplification in understanding power generally can produce parallel distortions in perceiving the effective use of power when applied to justice activism. What they often don't grasp is the way power in this context tends to only move in the modes of emotive self-expression or avant-garde revolutionary zeal. They want to advocate for change, but they are not exactly sure what that means and, as a result, they are not exactly sure what they're doing. In an image-saturated culture, power for these students often gets confused with a form of activism, change-agentism, or social-justice-warriorism devoid of a thick culture of relation and durable collective engagement. As Astra Taylor has suggested, this kind of activism and advocacy tends to privilege raising awareness (#18 on the list of "Things White People Like") and thinks of organizing only as putting together an event, creating a hashtag, or circulating a petition. These things are not bad, of course, but it will shock no one to realize that they are also relatively ineffective. Something I have had to learn and something I continue to try to teach my students is discussed by Taylor:

> It has always been easy for elites to dismiss those
> who challenge them as losers and malcontents,
> but it takes even less effort to ignore a meme.
> Successful organizers, by contrast, are more
> difficult to shrug off, because they have built
> a base that acts strategically. The goal of any
> would-be world-changer should be to be part of
> something so organized, so formidable, and so
> shrewd that the powerful don't scoff: they quake.[2]

Real power is not simply making noise or causing a commotion; it's not "giving the finger to The Man" or inviting Naomi Klein to town. It has to be something deeper, and this is even more the case for power theologically understood.

Within community organizing culture, power is the ability or capacity to do something, to act in some way "that causes a reaction." In other words, it is the capacity or ability to direct or influence other persons or the course of events. This distinguishes action that uses power from mere "activity," which often ignores power relations—an extremely significant distinction and dictum in IAF's training on organizing. Power is action and also the dynamic fabric of human relations—it's part of every relationship and human venture. Intrinsic to creation itself, power is naturally part of a living, moving world—especially a world that incorporates humans. It is energy, and as with energy, it's always there and can be built up, assembled, and directed. While each of us is likely all too familiar with the way this capacity is used by some to do wrong, pastor and community organizer Dennis Jacobsen reminds us that there is also a "biblical view of power that summons us to engage and to use power in ways that are creative, liberating, and life giving."[3] Within organizing, discussions on power tend to focus on two main sources: organized money and organized people. But obviously, for Christians, this is not the whole story. Power is ultimately God's, and the church is by nature essentially a reality of this power. While there's no doubt that power is exercised corruptly, and that it is often we who distort it, we should also recognize that God's creative power is what brings the church into existence and it is our mission to continue to participate in God's ongoing act of re-creation. This ability to do something is exactly at the heart of the church as a community and why it organizes people and resources. But what exactly the church is called to do and therefore how it is to engage in the exercise of power needs more clarification. For that, we want to look to the gospel.

The Power of Jesus

The problem many of our congregations have with power often plays out in how we see Jesus. Here, two polarities seem to dominate. On the one hand, Jesus is relegated to the figure of a simple wandering teacher, something of a utopian bucolic moralist. He offers token thoughts on how to be a better person, think positively, and live simply, but he's no more of a threat to the status quo than Mr. Rogers. On the other hand, and clearly in reaction to this domesticated vision, a machismo Jesus who cusses, drinks beer, pushes his way around, and knows how to "get things done" has become fashionable in certain circles. We (the authors) tend to think that both of these, however, misconstrue the person of Jesus. And while we have no desire to speculate on the personality of the historical Jesus per se, if we can begin to read the gospels with first-century ears we may in fact find a Jesus who is more complicated, compassionate, *and* dangerous. To do so, we turn to the oldest of the gospels, the gospel according to Mark, and Jesus' confrontation with the Gerasene demoniac (Mk. 5:1–17).

If you're familiar with Mark's gospel, you'll know that in Mark everything happens at breakneck pace and seems almost to be written in onomatopoeia. The gospel starts from the first line as something of a whirlwind. Even the term "gospel" smacks of controversy. Far from being a heartwarming segment to counterbalance an endless news cycle of scandal, crime, and violence, "good news" in the nomenclature of that time connotes something more akin to a report about the salvation of civilization or the defense or rescue of society from the threat of chaos or devastation. It usually is reserved for reporting on the realm-securing birth of a king or of his mighty and salvific acts on behalf of the people or empire. In the opening paragraphs we are alerted up front that this "good news" of Jesus is about power—that is, decisive actions and events. By Mark's staccato narrative, Jesus comes on the scene in a flash, directly on the heels of the erratic John the Baptizer's preaching. A quick baptism completed, the Spirit basically drags Jesus by the collar into the desert, where he is tempted. By the time we reach chapter five, he's already had a confrontation in the synagogue; he's performed healings; he's had multiple run-ins with the authorities; and he's apparently authorized himself to teach the people—more like an insurrectionary populist or a tent revivalist than a chaplain or bohemian. So, it's fair to say, Mark's not getting paid by the word to write this story, and it's much more of an action flick than a character piece.

This scene in chapter five does not detour from the pace or charge of the narrative to this point. As portrayed by Mark, Jesus is not a figure who hovers above the fray of power or simply eludes its force field. As our friend Rev. Kristin White put it, citing one of her favorite commentators, "*Game of Thrones* has nothing on the Bible."[4] Jesus is engaged here in a battle. He is immersed in a confrontation with a violent spirit, who's possessed this man and overpowered him such that no one can restrain him. In the imagery of the day, it's also clear that this clash is not simply one between two individuals but is illustrative of a larger conflict, a cosmic collision between two opposing powers.

Like the "Fool" from Shakespeare's *King Lear*, as Ched Myers has so lucidly described, the demoniac reveals the truth about the Roman Empire's oppressive reign, its occupation of Palestine, and its exploitation and domination of Israel. The confrontation in this scene, therefore, only furthers the *coup d'etat* that, as we've mentioned, begins the entire gospel. Mark's annunciation of "the good news of Jesus Christ, the Son of God" (1:1) is a direct attack upon the legitimacy and authority of the emperor (who was thought to be the son of God), and is a proclamation of a new reign, a new reality. The scene itself is saturated with battle and military imagery and terminology. Again, following Myers, we can begin to hear and see it with first-century ears and eyes. The "legion" (v. 9) of spirits inhabiting the demoniac is a term that only would have referred to a division of Roman soldiers in Mark's social world. This notion is further emphasized by the fact that the "herd" (v. 11) Jesus sends the spirits to enter is a bit of an odd term for referring to a group of pigs. The original word used is really a term for a band of military recruits. When Jesus grants the spirits permission to enter the swine (v. 13), the verb here is one that connotes a military command, something more like "he dismisses them," and consequently, the word used to describe the rushing of the pigs into the sea (v. 13) is really one used to describe a military "charge" into battle. Finally, of course, the drowning of "enemy troops" (the pigs) in the sea strongly echoes the drowning of Pharaoh's army back in Exodus, only solidifying the liberative theme of this text.

Jesus is no stranger to power. Indeed, his power is the heart of his message and work. However, this is not to say that Jesus' power operates just like everyone else's. We find Jesus in this gospel passage, as elsewhere, out on the edges of the society, on the margins of respectable culture, with the outcasts and the marginalized. It is here that he comes into confrontation with the established powers—who have control of things and want to keep them the way they are. As with earlier confrontations, Jesus' good news clashes with the oppressive authorities. His challenge to their dominion makes way for the new reality Jesus brings and aims to establish. To quote Myers:

> In Mark's narrative strategy, the synagogue and Gerasene exorcisms represent Jesus' inaugural challenge to the Powers. Put in military terminology, they signal the decisive breach in the defenses of the symbolic fortress of Roman Palestine. The political and ideological authority of both the scribal establishment and the Roman military garrison—the two central elements within the colonial condominium—have been repudiated. The narrative space has been cleared for the kingdom ministry to commence in full, both to Jew and to gentile.[5]

Jesus is no stranger to power, but his power is not the same as that of the empire or the system, nor will it work in the same manner.

Operating from the margins, Jesus engages these powers and confronts, resists, and defeats them, but he does so in a way that moves differently and exercises a unique kind of potency (which is the exact power of his gospel message). This is not to say that his active work is diluted or harmless. In fact, its cost will be great for some and its enactment will cause much trouble. However, its mode of operation—its way of working to include those on the margins, to offer hospitality, to liberate from bondage and captivity, to heal when economic logic suggests maintenance is more profitable, to move in compassion even to the point of loving an enemy—is also what contests those in power who benefit from the way things are. A new power intrinsic to a new form of relationship characterizes and comprises Jesus' ministry and mission. And it is this very relational (communion) power of the Spirit that he gives to his disciples, and that will be the substance of the way for those who follow him (Jn. 20:22; Acts 2). It's the inverted-style power Paul proclaims to the Corinthians, which can look like foolishness or even weakness and yet drives his ministry and through which, despite its seeming irrationality, God is actively transforming the world (1 Cor. 1:18–25). In Jesus, God is doing something: God is powerfully rectifying the human condition by gathering a newly restored and reconciled people.

A Newly Powered Church

It should be no shock to recognize that power is essential to forming healthy and vibrant congregations actively engaged in the mission of the church. Bill Easum recognizes that "stuck" congregations versus "unstuck" ones tend to embody different flows of power configured by their respective system stories. As with water flowing down a hill or across a valley, power tends to cut channels or grooves, and these ruts become the conduits through which it naturally moves from then on. To speak of the system story is to speak of these conduits—that is, the normal channels that have become the ruts of the congregation. It is "the way we've always done things," "how things normally happen here." It is those fall-back dynamics that tend to reassert themselves even when you attempt to restructure the organization. Stuck institutions repeat system stories that privilege top-down flows of power, regulating how the organization thinks and acts. Command and control are privileged, and this tends to stifle creativity, engagement, and risk-taking. Unstuck congregations, quite differently, develop system stories whose flows of power foster and encourage bottom-up, permission-giving, and entrepreneurial activities, instilling them with a cultural DNA that allows them to engage more vigorously in mission.[6]

While Easum may run the risk of failing to see the degree to which the church is itself the mission, and as a result, he possibly privileges a Christianity that may seem to be too tightly wound around individual faith, he rightly calls leaders to attend to the system stories that so often trap congregations. What he helps us see is that, within healthy and active congregations, power is often configured differently. Within "unstuck" congregations power flows more from the bottom up and is activated at what we normally take to be the margins–similar to what we saw above with Jesus in the gospel. No wonder vibrant communities are so unusual. In fact, one of the critical places to start in moving your congregation toward a newly organized community will be to ascertain how power flows within the congregation currently–to, as we might say, depict the system story.

My (Dan's) brother spent four years working for a parachurch ministry that specialized in coaching congregations through the adaptive challenges of our current context. The organization was innovative and offered some solid tools for helping congregations build strong cultures of discipleship and mission. In line with what we've been suggesting thus far, it recognized the need for collaborative leadership, co-governance, and creating a risk-taking, permission-giving climate. It even taught its clients how to begin to move in this direction. And yet, the ministry itself remained continually dominated by the central founding leader, who was never able to give up the reins of control. Eventually, as you might expect, it completely imploded because the other leaders, staff, and the entire organization could not withstand his continual violent overcorrections or his control-obsessed intrusions. In the end, nearly everyone left or were pushed out by his reckless intimidation and hostile takeovers of other people's projects.

Knowing that we need to move to decentralization, toward deprofessionalization, and to shared control does not make it easy to do, and neither does it make it happen. It's particularly not easy for clergy in an era of church decline, who thus already feel themselves threatened or, worse, obsolete. But as we have learned from our work in organizing, it's the only way forward if we're to cultivate vibrant communities empowered to embody the kingdom and to extend that vitality in mission. The organization and flow of power matters for a congregation, but many of us take little time to attend to how it operates or flows.

One of the basic practices of community organizing, due to its interest in power, is to conduct a power analysis. First, this is something done internally. A power analysis is not a flow chart, as flow charts tend to depict the ideal way decisions and operations proceed. Instead, a power analysis is a *real* depiction of the power dynamics within a committee, leadership team, ministry, or congregation. It seeks to provide a sense of who can make decisions and has influence, as well as to make clearer the allies and opponents within a given context or with respect to a certain initiative. It's probably easiest to describe by offering an illustration.

I (Tim) served many years as a pastor and elder at an iconic, medium-sized university town church that met originally in a campus building and then built its first facility right on the edge of campus. Having some roots in the creative and reactionary strands of evangelicalism that became prominent in the 1960s, this church had a unique and even revolutionary organizational structure: there was a flat leadership structure at the top involving all of the pastors and a group of volunteer lay elders. This team of paid and unpaid leaders worked by a strict consensus, meaning each person had the de facto freedom to veto any decision. A lay elder presided over the group, but did not hold any heightened authority. The compensation for the pastors was also strictly egalitarian, with the only differences in salary related to years of experience rather than value of one position over another. It was unique, and some said impossible, even though the church grew to over 1500 attenders during its ascent and became a bit of a cultural phenomenon with a deep, abiding loyalty from the many youthful members who departed in the natural transitions of a university community.

However, there was a constant disquiet, even among the elders and other deeply engaged leaders, about "how things actually got done." Despite the simple, flat, consensual design, this seemed to be a mystery, a mystery that produced great frustrations when people had new ideas or collective critique. So great was the accumulating frustration and eventually growing division (on theological and cultural grounds) that, despite the church's forty-year history of effective ministry, the church eventually reverted to a more traditional, authoritarian model and a strict, conservative dogmatic posture.

A power analysis renders some significant insights into the success, struggles, and eventual course of this congregation. The leadership structure closely paralleled that of a university department—with all its beauties *and* horrors. The system, like university departments in a tenure system, strongly encouraged autonomy, which often produced amazingly creative projects. It also made it extremely difficult to be efficient and enact boundaries or controls on initiatives that might have been tangential to the mission or on individuals who might have been divisive or simply used their personalities/gifts to run over the top of plans and processes that had been painstakingly created by others. And indeed, this was happening regularly. The result was that informal power, whether by creating artful expressions of worship or formation or by enacting destructive, selfish actions, was dominating the life of the community. This was embodied most in a larger-than-life founder, who was excessively gifted but struggled to acknowledge the informal power he exacted on decisions and the tone of the shared ministry. A common refrain from all of us in leadership was that we personally didn't hold the smoking gun of failed, painful, or unpopular decisions. Hence, dramatic frustrations at times were directed at the elders or deacons because they seemed the only authorities. In reality, they too were often being dominated by charismatic leaders outside the leadership structure exerting informal relational power on various processes. Without a power analysis, it was easy to champion the radical (and even biblical) nature of our structure without being able to understand the sources of our struggles and our limits. Most grievously, our self-observation and practice proceeded as if the only power present in the body was the power of God's Spirit—which primarily enlivened individuals in terms of generating authentic faith—without acknowledging any of the other types of power living within our fellowship.

Not only does a power analysis provide a better understanding of the dynamic and flow of power within your congregation, it also allows you to see where that structure might be stifling involvement or shutting down creative risk-taking.

When considering a church, it's essential to grasp the different kinds of power. There is, of course, the staple difference between "money power" and "people power." However, it's important to recognize there are also different kinds of power among people. First, there is the kind of power we typically think of in our society: power *over*. In this mode, as Ed Chambers describes, "[O]ne person's power is his or her ability to get someone else to do what he or she wants; the other person's power is to do as that person chooses. In power encounters, it's one against the other."[7] Here, power is a zero-sum game, with all of us trying to wield it over each other: Cain versus Abel. Second, there is a construal of power as power *for*. Much like the notion of power over, this view of power understands it to be competitive, except it emphasizes the practice of power as something that should be liberative for those who are being oppressed by powerful overlords (whether they be economic, ethnic, political, cultural, etc.). Usually associated with a strong leader, advocate, or activist, "power for" typically conceives of power in a way that those privileged to have it exercise it on behalf of those who do not. It's liberalism at its purest, but notice that it still conceives of and practices power as a zero-sum game. Finally, and this is the form of power cultivated within broad-based or congregational organizing, there is power *with*. To quote Chambers again, this is "relational power" that is "infinite and unifying, not limited and divisive." Being "additive and multiplicative" by nature, it grasps power not as simply pushing one's own interest but from joining with others in true solidarity—that is, reciprocal and mutual concern and care for each other.[8] One of the most important things we think we can learn for the future of ministry is to understand and practice power as *power with*.

Patterned on the ministry and work of Jesus, congregations that work to build grassroots power forged in solidarity and interdependence will find themselves further empowered by their receptivity to one another and to the work of the Spirit. Describing the potency of this kind of solidarity, Fr. Greg Boyle, playing on a Jesuit theme, describes how God animates us in such kinship: "Kinship—not in serving the other, but in being one with the other. Jesus was not 'a man for others'; he was one with them. There is a world of difference."[9] Liturgy is exactly where we learn and practice this revolutionary way of Jesus, a way that resonates strongly with the work of community organizing. Indeed, what we will describe in the remainder of this book are several practices for learning to build powerful grassroots congregations in a way that richly connects them with the worshiping life of the church. As with organizing, there is an amalgamating and catalytic power at work; only here we have stressed that the primary agent is the Spirit.

One of the first things, if not the first thing, you learn when you engage with organizing is the Iron Rule: "You never do for others what they can do for themselves." While this can sound quite cruel, especially to white middle-class ears, what it really communicates is that real, healthy communities are not the creation of single individuals, no matter how altruistic their intentions. Instead, it reminds us that the work of creating community is *community* work. And there's no doubt that moving in this direction is a bit chaotic by nature. Yet, we are starting to grasp that life in the church, not completely unlike the dynamics of physics, emerges not in static equilibrium, but on the edge of chaos. An organizational structure that seeks to develop this kind of power can be described by what Dee Hock calls "chaordic." As he explains, a chaord is "any self-organizing, self-governing, adaptive, nonlinear, complex organism, organization, community, or system, whether physical, biological, or social, the behavior of which harmoniously blends characteristics of both chaos and order."[10] To embrace a chaordic mode of leadership, then, is to relinquish control in order to create space for creativity, risk-taking, collective decision-making, vulnerable receptivity, and attentive listening. It may seem strange, but we think developing more vibrant and mobilized congregations will depend on our ability to cultivate chaordic communities.

The idea that the work of creating community is community work is even more true for the church. Indeed, this is exactly what the term "liturgy" implies—work of the people. The problem is that so often when it comes to our congregations, we default to alternative system stories associated with more efficient, controlled, or "successful" ways of doing things.

We have a friend who recently witnessed the remarkable empowerment that can come with moving from strong central control to a more decentralized and deprofessionalized (chaordic) mode of organization within his own youth ministry. For many years, his congregation had had a strong and extremely talented leader over the youth ministry. During this leader's tenure, the programs were unrivalled, the quality of teaching excellent, and the weekly meetings wonderfully creative and deeply engaging. Yet, as with many wonderfully talented individuals, this leader's strength and ability were also his weakness, as his perfectionism and true care for quality repeatedly led him to exclude and discount the involvement of other leaders. As a result, while the quality of the ministry remained high and even reached in unique ways a particular group of students who connected deeply with this leader, the ministry as a whole was only able to achieve a base level of vitality. Because everything flowed through the control of this strong central leader, other leaders were never developed and the relational culture of the ministry did not grow. As a result, the great majority of students never became strongly knitted into the fabric of the ministry, didn't receive close mentorship, and never became active in the ministry other than functioning as a passive audience. What our friend's congregation discovered, once this strong leader moved on, was that a large space opened up for a youth ministry team that brought together a diverse group of leaders with new ideas, more energy, and greater ability to connect relationally with a larger portion of the students. The result has been a complete change. The youth ministry now, while a bit more chaotic, is substantially more vibrant, as more students are fully engaged and actively involved, growing in their own discipleship, their sense of mission, and learning to embrace their own gifts in leadership.

When we embody a community of solidarity by recognizing one another's gifts in ways that identify and multiply leaders–fostering mutual accountability that takes our baptismal vows seriously, listening to the wisdom of each person through attending to each voice, and working to discern together through forgiveness–we build a culture of permission-giving and interconnectivity that empowers our people beyond what's possible under centralized control. A new kind of energy emerges from the bottom up that is multiplicative, unifying, self-catalyzing, and entirely resonant with the church's ethos and nature. An empowered community of co-laborers and fellow-ministers can emerge. Continuing to nurture grassroots congregational organization through such practices strengthens its resiliency and ability to resist the tendency within social movements toward stale bureaucracy and centralized management that sociologist Robert Michels memorably called "the iron law of oligarchy."[11] Characteristic of churches and faith communities committed to an organizing structure and faithful to its practices is that they build relational power. In so doing, they cultivate solidarity while identifying, recruiting, and training new and diverse leaders. Additionally, they promote reconciling dialogue that allows them to attend to the movement of the Spirit within a permission-giving context while encouraging collective discernment through active listening. Such an approach invigorates the congregation internally and activates it for mission. Organized this way, our people become empowered and our congregations become powerful!

Power to Engage the Powers

Part of many churches' baptismal covenant is a vow to "renounce the evil powers of this world that corrupt and destroy the creatures of God." And even congregations that don't include this in their formal baptismal liturgy (or don't have a formal baptismal liturgy) teach their people that integral to their call to be part of God's people is to not be conformed to the world (Rom. 12:2), to have died to the world's way of operating (Col. 2:20), and to have been enlivened in Christ's freedom to embody an alternative (Eph. 2:1–7). Being joined to the body of Christ, in the early church's self-understanding, implied coming into conflict with the "principalities and powers" that ruled the world. A discussion of the place of power in the church, therefore, cannot be complete without describing how its power engages the systems and forces that order our society and the globe.

The notion of Powers that exercise dominion over our lives may, at first blush, seem a bit outlandish or primitive–figments of an overactive imagination or a worldview too influenced by *The Lord of the Rings, Harry Potter,* or, worse, the genre of spiritual fiction. But what the New Testament writers seem to have in mind when they refer to these entities are the forces, institutions, ideologies, or symbols that give structure to our lives, conduct a certain ordering function, and seem to possess the ability to make things happen. While these were originally part of the good creation of God, as the New Testament writers convey, they are now fallen and act in rebellion, exercising their dominion in ways that distort and corrupt human life. Where they should serve to mediate our relation to God and one another, working for our good and incorporating us into God's love, they now enslave and harm us, leaving us lost.[12] Operating beyond our control, these systems and structures perpetuate brokenness, exploitation, oppression, division, hostility, and death, establishing under their sovereignty these patterns and rivalries.

It doesn't take much imagination in our day to grasp what some of these Powers might be. Nazism, terrorism, slavery, and human trafficking quickly come to mind; but then so do such things as money, international markets, nation states, laws, and technology– with varying degrees of decadence. They need not embody the fullest extent of evil in order for us to recognize the way Powers exert their influence upon our lives in ways that contest God's good intentions for us. Take money and financial markets, for instance. Few of us can forget, and many of us are still reeling from, the economic crisis of 2008. That Wall Street (while not exactly referring to a specific person or persons) exerts a certain power over our society, and that its workings have a real impact on our lives, is obvious. Similarly, the markets associated with Wall Street also give a certain pattern to our decisions and activities. It was deemed a wise decision by nearly everyone to purchase a house in 2005; no broker, financial planner, official, or executive was declaring mortgages irresponsible or foolish. Indeed, home purchases were the backbone of the economy, the main source of individual wealth, and widely promoted as a sure, smart investment. When the reality behind securities and derivatives, adjustable rate mortgages, and sub-prime lending practices was revealed, however, and the market imploded, U.S. households and people across the globe felt the ramifications. Millions of homes were lost to foreclosure; trillions of dollars of personal wealth and retirement funds evaporated; unemployment skyrocketed, as did poverty. Meanwhile, those in the know, having bet against the system they set up, walked away with billions and billions of dollars. All of it was the fallout of a distorted and corrupt structure of financial products, regulation failure, and collective greed that wreaked devastation across the globe while lining the pockets of a few—as massive an instance of accumulation by dispossession as has ever occurred.

Recalling the way of Jesus we described at the beginning of this chapter, it is only fitting that the community of those gathered in following him will in turn seek to oppose these distorted structures and forces, especially with particular attention to the most oppressed in their subjection to them. In this way we can begin to see that the church does not have a mission that is disconnected from its own internal life, but instead—as it embodies its unique power of joining with one another in Christ by the Spirit—it already is performing its mission. The very effect of this new community's presence and action is to put it in conflict with the corrupted Powers and principalities that sustain their power through exploitation, violence, and oppression. The community of the church is a power-base for engaging the Powers that dominate the world, but, as we have seen, it is a counterpower not cut from the same cloth, nor does it operate in the same way.

In the freedom opened up by Christ's defeat of the Powers in the cross, the church can act as a power to engage these destructive Powers, living first as a witness to an alternative and then operating as a counterpressure in service to the world. This is not "do-goodery" or only loosely connected social responsibility, but it is the very act of mobilization in mission itself. A community gathered under the lordship of Christ and embodying his way will naturally seek to make known and extend this restored reality. In freedom, however, its mode of engagement will be distinct from that of the Powers of the world, even as it will be wise to the Powers' operations. In our experience, congregation-based community organizing has offered one robust channel for such missional engagement as these organizations work to further solidarity through relationships and to build more just and healthy communities. Such engagements recognize the reality of power, making use of external power analyses to expose the structure. Relying on creatively nonviolent tactics, they perform a kind of jujitsu in their work that tends to defang these powers, often playing on their own tendency to overextend themselves in ways that lead to their own undoing. Hence, congregations involved in these local and relational organizations can discover in them a resonant culture for collaboration that compounds their own missional activity and extends it into the wider society. When attended to theologically, and with constant connection to their worshiping life, churches involved in community organizing become power-bases through whom the reign of God ripples out in waves of solidarity and political engagement to contest and challenge the distorted dominion of these structural Powers. Acting in this way, even small congregations can have a powerful impact, becoming uniquely powerful communities of formation and mission.

You've likely heard that one of the trends in multinational business is the practice of inversion, through which large corporations evade taxes by locating their "headquarters" (which might simply be a P.O. box) in the Cayman Islands or some other tax haven. It's a practice of these Powers that only serves to further the way they escape accountability and oversight, or shirk their relationships to the local community so as to maximize more profits. Well, we like to think that our congregation, Emmaus Way, exemplifies an inversion of its own, but in almost an opposite manner because it's a missional inversion. What we mean by this is that our congregation, while rather small in numbers and having no facilities of our own, has had a disproportionate impact on our local community because of the way we've organized power. Unlike large or big-steeple congregations that may have much influence on their local communities through their connections to officials and power brokers on the city council, or through just their mere dominance of the downtown skyline, our people have been self-mobilized to engage multiple, formidable campaigns— working with ex-offenders struggling to reenter society, supporting local artists, impacting city decisions and planning on affordable housing, pressing Duke University to provide living wages, caring for refugees resettled in our area, leading the charge against a race-based policing culture that ultimately led to the end of our Police Chief's tenure, standing against the discriminatory laws of the state legislature, and even engaging Bank of America Company over foreclosures and interest rates. We often joke that we are something of a hobbit as a community, given that our footprint is much larger than would be expected from such a small and unassuming congregation.

We should be clear: our community has not always been in complete agreement about some of this work. As with any congregation, some of our people have felt more passionately about one of these issues than others; others have reserved judgment on some of these initiatives even as solidarity with the poor and marginalized is something all of our people believe is central to the practice of communion. However, since we have used the tools of organizing, we have been able to build a relational culture that is permission-giving, decentralized, and deprofessionalized such that our people have felt empowered and encouraged enough to risk following the Spirit's lead with the assurance that together the community will try to help each other understand the work in light of the gospel. At the same time, we have found in our work with congregations through organizing networks that our collaborative efforts resound with a potency far beyond what our small congregation on its own could muster.

While churches often decline to talk about power, presuming it is beneath their moral view of themselves to consider it, organizing has taught us to attend to power and to focus on building it in a particular way in our congregation. Power matters! As congregations on the way to reanimation and mobilization, we must be returned to the power of Jesus Christ in the Spirit, learning how to cultivate and embody it. Not only will this invigorate our discipleship, but it will also greatly enliven our mission. As we might say—amid a world of exploitation, gruesome disparities, arrogance, greed, lies, and abuse—no longer can we be satisfied to be a lame church, "holding to the outward form of godliness but denying its power" (2 Tim. 3:5).

4

RE-CONNECTING the Church: The Constructive Practice of the Relational Meeting

It's Tuesday morning in East Baltimore. More specifically, it's "Turnaround Tuesday." The basement of Zion Baptist Church is crowded with around sixty persons, most if not all of them self-identified as former offenders, all seeking a sustainable life in a society now so powerfully closed to them. They are sitting in rows of folding chairs facing a small podium, a randomly placed collection of whiteboards and chalkboards, and the small stage so characteristic of church basement fellowship halls. Despite this scene that recalls countless support group meetings, potlucks, talent shows, and fundraisers known to almost any urban churchgoer, there is something entirely different happening in this space. The mood is contagiously upbeat; there is a physical sense of both resolve and hope in the room that outdistances the pride of many parents who have surely crowded into this space to watch their children perform. The clients in this room, despite past mistakes, are on a rigorous and sure path to living-wage jobs at Johns Hopkins Medical Center and some of Baltimore's other most respected institutions.

When the testimonies start, one powerfully built man begins with a matter-of-fact declaration of his thirty-three years of incarceration. Upon release, his plan was to play it straight for a couple weeks, but then he knew he would have to "get a gun" because he would "need to eat." Instead, somewhat miraculously, he found his way into the affirmation, support, and training of Turnaround Tuesdays, and weeks later he successfully interviewed for a living-wage job. My

[Tim's] tears and the tears of others around the room are now flowing freely as he reports the pride and dignity he felt in informing family members of his employment and his newfound ability to contribute.

It's another remarkable scene witnessed by Durham CAN's Clergy Caucus team on the trip to visit our sister organization in Baltimore. Not lost in this scene, despite the power of these testimonies, is a group of ten or more volunteers and community organizers from Baltimoreans United in Leadership Development (BUILD) moving, smiling, greeting, and meeting with clients on the periphery with an obvious relational ease. Just a few weeks removed from the riots and protest in the wake of Freddie Gray's death, a police officer sits on stage exuding familiarity with the program and friendship with many of those present—clients and volunteers alike. The marks of so many deeply nurtured relationships were delightful to note, but could also be easily minimized with respect to their role in the astonishing work currently being done in the city. As the day progressed, we learned how significant an oversight that would be.

When partnered with their astounding work on affordable housing, this effort on living-wage jobs is a great vision of hope in a context that can only be characterized as despairing. To put the impact of BUILD's initiatives in perspective, it's worth remembering that during the Great Depression U.S. unemployment hovered around 25 percent. In this part of Baltimore, only a short walk from the dazzling Inner Harbor, the postindustrial collapse of the city left unemployment at a staggering 55 percent.[1] In later reflection, our team all acknowledged that we had seen a vision of God's gracious kingdom being enacted, the "great economy" so fondly named by Wendell Berry, where a community blighted by contention and loss was being regenerated in a vision of the "shalom/rest" commonly characterized in Hebrew theology and readily taken up by Jesus.[2] We were on holy ground and we knew it. These scenes comprise some of the hope and outcomes that all people of faith desperately desire to see, join, and generate.

We eagerly asked the organizers and pastors who were our hosts how so much had been done by so few. Their reply was startling and simple—relationships. There was a deep relational context to the work that resulted in thousands of beautifully restored homes in East Baltimore and the establishment of living-wage jobs for those who had formerly offended. These stunning kingdom outcomes were embedded in a carefully nurtured web of relationships that engendered the trust, courage, creativity, and collaboration to catalyze and complete this work. Real relationships had been cultivated among organizers, pastors, congregations, neighbors, eventual investors, developers, job providers, job seekers, renters, homebuyers, and even potential antagonists to these projects. The relational work throughout this whole project was intentional, pervasive, and courageous.

The jobs program began when pastors and organizers regularly approached persons on the corners selling illegal drugs in their community. They asked what it would take to get them off the corners and began hearing what would become a consistent answer—jobs! The vast majority of these dealers readily expressed that they would strongly prefer dignified and sustainable work to the dangers and risks of this illegal trade. Local church leaders and organizers quickly formed a simple conclusion: Baltimore's crime problem was really a jobs problem! This realization was a bold counter-narrative (though one not without serious sociological support)[3] to what has become a dominant, contemporary cultural story that vilifies the poor, accentuates the criminality of the young and the unemployed, and demands a heavy-handed response of criminal interdiction to scourge these problem individuals.

The transformative power of relationships characterized by trust, dialogue, and mutual interest is a reality known by most church and organizational leaders. We experience the lasting impact of the presence or absence of relational trust and relational processes almost daily. Our own fellowship faced a crossroads decision after our first five years as a community, having outgrown our small, beautiful, and much-loved storefront in downtown Durham. Two options emerged. On the one hand, we had been invited to consider sharing some space at a historic downtown church. Our other possibility was to become tenants in the building of a failed church that was now owned by another ministry. The first option offered the beauty, stability, administrative support, recognition, bureaucratic realities, and complicated historical legacy expected of most established churches. Since our fellowship was and remains deeply influenced by liturgy and tradition, there were some obvious attractions to this location. The second option would establish us as tenants of and partners with a new missional organization that was, like all new organizations—including us—struggling with sustainability and constantly redefining its program and mission. The space this second partner offered was a beautiful, large, hardwood, high-ceilinged open space that doubled as a youth recreation space during the week. In other words, it was a blank canvas, albeit with a few sneaker marks, that would effectively require us to entirely change our logistics by needing to move in and move out all of our seating, art, and sound equipment each week. It was a crossroads decision for our community.

Church planters will instantly recognize the acute vulnerability of this moment. Space decisions not only radically change the fragile rhythms of new churches but also often redefine their missions and are the critical factors in their sustainability. As you well know, form is content! In this case, our choices were radically different, and we clearly knew that the result would have an immeasurable impact on our future. (Six years later, this has proven to be entirely true.) Our default practice in decision-making was to talk and listen to each member in a sustained series of one-to-one meetings. The initial result of this process was frightening. We had no idea what we would say to and hear from each other, but our earliest conversations revealed our worst fears. Key leaders and staff were evenly divided, with strongly held preferences regarding the two spaces. Given the passionate nature of our community, there should have been little surprise that there were many strong, cogent opinions with very little moderation to be found.

The stakes were high. What do communities do when their passions are divided? In our case, we were able to rely on a process of dialogue and listening that guided the community toward decision and collaborative action in a highly nurtured context of participation where we deeply valued differences in personal story and experience. It was our relational fabric that allowed us to navigate this possibly treacherous territory. Without a thick relational culture, we might have been torn apart.

How to form a relational culture through dialogue and listening in relational meetings is the topic of this chapter, but first we must look at some very important changes in our social world that make these practices so transformative for communities. Why is the work of relationship building so necessary? Though the specific practices we will describe might feel different and a bit alien, asserting the necessity of a relational process to the country church I [Tim] grew up in five decades ago, despite its faults, would be received as ridiculously obvious and unnecessary. What has changed and continues to change in the social life of our society that makes the imperative of a relational practice timely, necessary, and—dare we say—creative?

Relational Decline in a Hyper-Connective Culture

To state the obvious: communication connectivity in social lives over the last two decades has exploded beyond the imaginations of all but the most technologically prescient. Most of us are constantly sending and receiving messages. While I (Tim) write on my laptop this afternoon, I am following and contributing to text threads with my daughter, my son, and several groups of friends on my phone, while also cheating my writing time by intermittently checking various new media outlets on my iPad about today's latest (outrageous) election year hijinks. Hence, sitting alone in my public university office, which has no landline phone service, I am processing literally hundreds of communications. Roughly twenty years ago, without the use of a fixed telephone, I would be writing entirely in solitude. Yet, in another sense, I am still entirely alone!

Many researchers and social critics have strongly asserted that, despite this radical increase in connectivity, we are increasingly alone and disconnected in our technological society. How many of us, especially in the professional class, leave our homes daily by accessing a car in a closed garage and then driving directly to our work sites in sealed vehicles listening to a media of choice? Upon exiting our cars, we might put in ear buds to listen to self-generated media and arrive at our desks, cubicles, or even closed offices without any human interaction. How many of us taking public transit pop in those same ear buds and try to ignore one another?

Harvard demographer Robert Putnam in *Bowling Alone* led a chorus of other scholars trumpeting this conjoined phenomenon of heightened connectivity or activity with increased social isolation. In describing this reality, Putnam describes first the declining memberships by individuals in various civic groups and organizations. Then, using the metaphor that provides his title to further illustrate this point, Putnam explains that, while the activity of bowling has increased in the last few decades, membership in bowling leagues has simultaneously decreased. We bowl, but we bowl alone.[4] Of course, there is more at work here than simply social isolation. During these decades, informal social groups and communities have become durable and beloved aspects of our social landscape such that the term "community" often takes on a wide range of sacred and near-sacred meaning. Sociologist Robert Bellah and colleagues notably described our society's deep, historical commitment to individualism alongside the emergence in emotive value of various informal communities. Some of these informal communities are misshapen associations that bend some of the healthy attributes of community life. Using the term "lifestyle enclaves," they noted that many of these groupings and connections are centered on consumption and homogenous socioeconomic statuses that secure common lifestyles and hence assure the absence of the diversity that is part of the pleasant and painful reality of community life.[5] Gated subdivisions, running clubs, the Greek system in universities, alumni groups, and churches—especially churches—often illustrate these types of enclaves that only approximate the rich diversity, shared history, and collective future of authentic communities.

Hence, the personal isolation in a culture of constant messaging can be compensated for by the often pleasurable social interactions afforded in lifestyle enclaves.[6] Even in the most comfortable enclaves, there are some profound and dangerous voids. Personal needs and wounds can be left to fester in isolation. Equally, personal capabilities and gifts that could be a great blessing to many are often not recognized or bestowed. The absence of diversity in cultural life is dangerously viral. Structural inequities and structural racism are obscured, unspoken, and rendered taboo. The beautiful diversities of our social landscape are typically localized in a homogeneity that blunts the transformative power of our differences.

As previously alluded to, churches and other faith communities are often patrons of this dangerous arrangement. Gladly, we see many faith communities challenging this predicament with a variety of strategies, including the planting of multiracial churches, the revitalization of struggling or stagnant fellowships through diversification, and the recovery of the sense of the local parish in some ministries with the intentional goal of reflecting the mosaic of differences, needs, and diversities in their broader communities.[7] Nevertheless, particularly the white church in our society remains far too stratified socioeconomically and is, by definition, a reflection of and often an unwittingly bulwark to the dominant racial paradigm. Many colleagues leading traditionally black churches and denominations report a far greater economic diversity. But they also, with frustration, describe a delocalizing trend in their churches in which the points of attraction of shared life are charismatic preaching, prominent leaders, scale of ministry, and effective programs rather than deep commitments to a specific local neighborhood or even a common city.[8]

There are many relational reverberations associated with the changes noted in Putnam and Bellah and colleagues–and through our own observations. Recall Putnam's exemplar of heightened leisure activity, such as bowling, concurrent with the decline of participation in formal bowling leagues. He noted the marked decline in participation in organizations such as unions, fraternal organizations, PTAs, scouts, and a variety of civic groups. These social institutions once served as key cogs to the communal glue of social life in our society. This doesn't mean, to follow the analogy, that informal friendship groups aren't gathering–and often–to engage in some collective activity. But the dynamics of the informal friendship group, the type of groups noted by Bellah et al., are quite different from participation in an organized league. Governmental scholar Hugh Heclo emphasizes that these marked changes impact not only the dynamics of social activity but, perhaps even more importantly, how we think about social and community life. He demarcated a decisive difference between *thinking about institutions* from the outside (a frame of reference that can be simply bureaucratic and organizationally myopic) and *institutional thinking*–that is, thinking about institutions from within and hence seeing oneself as a social or even a moral agent with significant social connections and obligations.[9]

To use an analogy of family life, this distinction is all the difference in the world between thinking abstractly, academically, and perhaps even benevolently about the concept of family and thinking about familial responsibilities, possibilities, and challenges within the context of a specific family. His words on institutional thinking and the consequences of their absence are significant and merit a lengthy quote:

> If our teaching considers institutions from only an outside, external viewpoint, we reinforce the prevailing tendency to dismiss the meaningfulness of institutional values. Understanding from the inside lets us see how people use such value commitments to appraise their own and others' behavior, to give reasoned meaning to the decisions and actions that they take in life. By omitting the internal point of view, we indirectly teach and reinforce the idea *that our social existence is merely a succession of fluid, revocable associations of convenience and arbitrary personal tastes.*[10] (emphasis added)

That's what we're up against. The absence of institutional thinking partially explains low volunteerism turnout, endless church shopping, and incessant battles over worship or preaching styles. It helps explain what happens when the church succumbs to commodification. It does not take arduous observation to see how deeply our society cherishes individualism and how intensely protective we are about what we perceive to be our rights or preferences. Using Heclo's language, a lack of institutional thinking, specifically the inability for individuals to see themselves as internal to and intimately connected with communities and social organizations, warps and stunts the types of relationships we're forming in organizations—including churches. We lose a sense of "the commons," shared life enmeshed in durable social networks, and the kinds of relational commitments that make these commons possible. In many cases, churchgoers can see themselves primarily as individuals with personal relationships with God in a collective that protects those relationships and their rights and/or desires to worship along sets of specific personal preferences. In such cases, the primary orientations become the individuals rather than the church as a distinct presence of God's Spirit. Relationships with other worshipers can be supportive, friendly, and even deeply caring, but they are not decisively necessary, since the primary space of engagement with God is perceived to be the individual. In contexts that fully or partially exhibit these attributes, the practice of reweaving a thick relational fabric in order to create a relational culture does indeed become radical and transformative.

Let's now move to fuller discussion of this practice.

The One-to-One Relational Meeting

One of our core practices is what we call the "relational meeting," a term we have happily gleaned from our faith-based organizing training with IAF. We have adopted this language because it denotes a historically and intentionally thick practice that differs substantively from typical (also important) church encounters, such as visitations, pastoral counseling, accountability or encouragement meetings, spiritual direction, or discipleship/mentoring dyads. Instead, the relational meeting is intended distinctly to establish or broaden the relational commitment between individuals and to strengthen the relational fabric within a common community. In other words, relational meetings are simultaneously personal and communal. Applied specifically to faith-based communities, relational meetings should embody the theology/worldview of the community and hence, in process and outcome, should strengthen the relational and lived outcomes of that theology. For example, our community has been deeply formed by a practice of weekly dialogue (substituting for the traditional sermon) rooted in a strong theological tradition that recognizes the presence of God's loving presence and speech in all persons. In other words, similar to defining the "where" of the church mentioned earlier, our fellowship is deeply invested in commitments to the gifting of all persons of the fullness in Christ. Hence, relational meetings are critical in reinforcing this theological/communal allegiance and identity by intentionally seeking the voice and story of others in our community.

Moving to the specifics, relational meetings differ from other one-on-one meetings because they have a unique set of goals. A dominant, clear goal is to foster and reinforce community commitments. The relational meeting always seeks to build a stronger bond of relationships within a community, meaning that within each individual meeting there is an eye toward the whole and the forging of its common good. Given this goal of a common good, we often encourage relational meetings to be sought outside of one's primary network of friends and regular contacts. This avoids the echo chamber effect of already established friends restating common interests and perspectives that were likely the source of these friendship networks in the first place. In addition to the obvious benefit of enabling new connections, intentional meetings outside one's primary network also have the unique capability of promoting more relational meetings in their wake because they offer new information, unique perspectives, and fresh experiences that feed a greater curiosity to seek out other persons one does not know well.

Following this emphasis on the community, relational meetings build the community by motivating persons to action in specific social contexts. Hence, the practice involves hearing and sharing mutual interests, desires, and even a shared sense of anger related to specific social issues in order to set the stage for mutual, cooperative action. Collective action is a primary outcome, which is why relational meetings are staples in community organizing. Relational meetings also seek to identify new leaders necessary for building the community, guiding it into action, and sustaining it in the future.

With these goals in mind, from both training and experience, we have developed a series of effective practices for relational meetings (though these meetings are anything but scripted). IAF teaches that relational meetings are the most important actions of any leader. My (Tim's) new colleague and co-pastor at Emmaus Way, Molly Brummett Wudel, arrived this year at Emmaus Way with a strong IAF background. Her very first act as a pastor/leader in our community was to open her schedule for relational meetings. She assiduously avoided some of the accumulated tasks and urgencies that await any new leader to make relational meetings her primary focus for her first months. The outcome of this practice can hardly be overestimated. Even though she is enormously gifted and would have inevitably garnered great respect, I have never seen a gifted leader cultivate so much credibility and cull so much institutional knowledge in a diverse community so quickly. A first practice that we recommend is not only to create space for relational meetings, but to set very specific, accountable, and numerical goals you intend to achieve on a weekly and monthly basis. We (the co-pastors) both maintain goals for our volume of relational meetings and a list of specific persons in our communities we want to seek out. In our community organizing work, we try to have three to five meetings a week.

A second key practice is to be timely and to keep relational meetings fairly brief. In a greater civic setting, we try to keep meetings to thirty minutes. In a church setting, in which there is inevitably some bleed-over of conversation into other topics due to familiarity (though it is good to politely avoid too much of this), we strive to keep meetings to an hour. As is a very strong dictum in IAF and other organizing circles, we ardently try to start and end meetings on time. A reputation for timeliness and respect of time powerfully enhances one's ability to secure meetings with persons you don't know well.

The meeting itself orients around several critical questions. Naturally, as one would expect, we start with safer, personal narrative questions ("What brought you to this community? Where do you focus your time in this fellowship or community?") that explore aspects of this person's story with which you are not familiar. But then the conversation moves to the interests, passions, and issues that drive this person, which are commonly misunderstood in organizing circles and even more so when congregations interface with organizing practices. Interests are not crude, selfish desires. They are also not surface-level wishes or niceties, though often people will start here. Instead, interests are the deep hungers and motivating cares inherent to a person and her or his story. What experiences or issues have been deeply formative to this person's fidelities and passions? What changes does he or she want to make in your fellowship or the local community? These questions set the stage for the two most important questions—"Why?" and "Why?" In a relational meeting, you are avidly seeking the roots of a person's passions and often how this person has interpreted the key events in her or his life. The second "Why?" is critical because people often don't share these foundational reflections at the first ask, fearing either the vulnerability of the topic or assuming the usual superficial and perfunctory expectations. Moving past the niceties is critical to better understand what moves and impassions a person.

Besides asking good questions, the one who initiated the encounter should still remember that the goal of the meeting is a two-way conversation. This give-and-take not only enhances vulnerability but also works to build the relational connection that becomes an antecedent to both thicker community and shared action. We recommend listening for about two-thirds of the meeting and sharing the other third as a flexible ideal. Develop your own style for relational meetings. It's an art, not a science or mathematical formula. Practicing and honing a style that suits your story, positions, and personality will only enhance the authenticity of these meetings. But as you consider your own story and experiences, be careful to make sure these meetings are not dominated by your own personal issues and hang-ups. You are not there to push your agenda, and be forewarned that many folks will sniff this out quickly if you are. Similarly, there is certainly an evaluative element to relational meetings, but they are not designed to be judgmental. So, suspend your judgment and assiduously avoid measuring your meeting partner with by own issues and expectations.

Considering this evaluative element, we have been taught—and this was quite difficult to embrace initially—that relational meetings are "an action" directed at the person you have sought out. This is classic organizing language. In community organizing, community groups construct public actions to "agitate" and initiate a reaction from specified targets. We gather public officials or persons seeking public office and ask them direct questions about issues that the community whom we represent values in order to provoke a response and a reaction. We also develop actions by gathering our organized base, displaying the power of our voices, and giving an organized power to voices that are often ignored to confront and agitate formal leaders in our community who hold positional power and access. Every response, positive or negative, to gathered power becomes an impetus for future organizing and action.

Negative responses can define future action. For example, in a very recent public action in Durham, school board members, who were facing a $15 million budget shortfall, were disappointed to say "no" to a request from youth we had organized in our community regarding the hiring of additional school guidance counselors. The students, having conducted listening sessions (a process we take up in the next chapter) with other students throughout the community and having done stringent research on current staffing, made a compelling case.The board's public response of "no" was painful to its members, powerfully defining future actions and negotiations with the school board. After the public action, the school board was highly motivated to work with our county commissioners (who were also present at this public accountability session) and ultimately found the resources residing in a local community college fund that will allow for the hiring of additional college advisers! The action provoked a desired reaction even when the initial action exposed a negative. And naturally, positive responses build unity and the resolve for future action on particular issues. Organizing on public issues requires pushing on even those who might be sympathetic just as much as it means welcoming the efforts of those who have sided against us in the past.

All of this is equally true in the relational meeting. By asking about a person's personal narrative and passions, you are provoking and seeking a reaction. It is indeed an "action" directed at the person sitting across from you. You are discerning whether this person is a leader, and determining the level of leadership she or he can provide on specific issues or within a specific community context such as your church or fellowship. It is crucial to discern whether this person is a complainer, a passive critic, or a doer! Questions such as, "What have you done about this?" or, "Why haven't you done anything about this?" and, "Are you ready to now act on this concern?" become staples for this portion of the relational meeting. One learns a great deal, and the stage can be set for future relational action, even when the responses to these questions are deemed negative. But we strive to end relational meetings with a mutually agreed upon action. This could mean a commitment to meet again, to join an initiative, connect with other persons, study/read a relevant text, or collaborate on an area of shared passion exposed in the meeting.

As we have stressed, the relational meeting is not just an encounter between two individuals; it fortifies and expands the relational web of the community by advancing its missional/social agenda. Action is critical to these goals. It need not be grandiose, but leaving the meeting with a next step—even if it is merely a commitment to meet with another member—is crucial.

Though the resolution to act concludes the actual meeting, the final step is evaluation. We have had this essential and easily ignored lesson impressed upon us constantly in organizing culture. Particularly in IAF, after every relational meeting, listening session, internal caucus, or public action, we evaluate. We'll pick up this need for constant reevaluation in the concluding chapter of this book. But in the context of the relational meeting, our habit is to pause, reflect, and take a few notes after every meeting. What is this person's leadership potential? What about this person's story, actions, thoughtfulness, passions, and anger affirms that evaluation? What passions and loyalties does this person deem critically important, and will he or she take action on those? What is this person's relational network? Who else should I meet within that network? Who should I introduce this person to? How did this meeting go? What questions should I have asked, but somehow omitted? These are among the primary questions we thoughtfully ponder in our post-meeting evaluations.

In our community life at Emmaus Way, we have tried to build a relational meeting culture in which these encounters occur naturally and regularly in the life of the community. We mention this norm regularly in our weekly gatherings, encouraging our congregants to initiate relational meetings and respond to the initiation of others. But we also have a few intentional habits we believe support this culture of relationality. We have seasons of community listening (explained in the following chapter) and we complement each season of listening sessions with a community commitment to a heightened practice of relational meetings. Though a small congregation, we have a constant inflow of guests and new persons. These very intentional seasons of a heightened commitment to relational meetings become a great time for our community to reach out to and hear the stories of newcomers, learning how we might be shaped by their presence and participation. We also incorporate space within our weekly gathering for relational encounters. We extend the peace of Christ each week in a conversational time that is often more than five minutes. Our weekly practice of the Eucharist is also framed as a time of intentional relational encounter. Modeling the Eucharist meals of the early church, we serve each other, and do so in a manner in which there is space to engage the lives and stories of our community. It is a time of embracing, serving, remembering, encouraging, and interceding.

These highly relational moments in our weekly gathering are easily extended to allow for full relational meetings in the worship gathering, and we do so more than occasionally. The time is highly valued and cherished. We strongly anticipate you can and will find ways that will fit comfortably in the life of your community to encourage and sustain this practice. And we suspect that relational meetings, when made authentic to your community's unique life, will become equally valued.

Our understanding of the relational meeting and its basic components comes from long experience, the wisdom of others, and the benefit of excellent training. We have offered a strong template, coming from many great teachers. But we also want to be clear that the relational meeting is also an art that should be crafted and honed with deep sensitivity to many contexts, including the personality and style of the leader who initiates these meetings, the uniqueness of the person who is sought out, and the specific contexts that frame the relationship. For example, does this relationship originate in a faith community, a local township, a civic organization, a defined political entity, or a hybrid combination of multiple contexts? This is a point we want to emphasize: there are some unique qualities of relational meetings originating primarily in a church or faith community context. In local organizing, much of the energy and politic of a relational meeting might be sourced in anger, passion, and the desire for pointed change in a community. These are all certainly present in an ecclesial setting. But there is also a theological history and logic in the ecclesial context that sets boundaries, makes demands, and invigorates deep, imaginative possibilities for the relational meeting. To this point, it would be easy to see the instrumental and pragmatic possibilities of this practice. Surely, intentional, careful listening and the buttressing of a relational fabric would enrich the congregational life of any community. However, there is far more at play in the commitment to sustain a relational meeting culture in a congregation. There is a deep theological, ecclesiological rationale that not only propels this practice, but also, in turn, is thickened and formed by the practice of relational meetings. In other words, relational meetings are what churches should do given their theological history, *and* churches can better recognize themselves as churches formed in a distinct theological identity by this sustained practice. Remembering the second chapter, on ecclesiology, let's consider some of the theological connections to relational meetings and some of the unique aspects of a relational meeting culture in congregations.

The Relational Meeting as Theological Practice

In 2009, Father Jim Manship of St. Rose of Lima Roman Catholic Church in New Haven, Connecticut, found himself in the center of a storm of racialized policing. The local police had become a constant presence parked outside of Latino-owned businesses. Standard practice included profiling the customers and being vigilant for minor vehicle issues or any other cause to initiate police stops and harassing searches. Business at these locations plummeted in response. Ultimately, while filming two police officers who had entered a convenience store and were indiscriminately seizing a merchant's property, Father Manship was arrested.[11] The arrest of the prominent priest sparked a long cycle of defiant community organizing that initiated federal civil rights action, yielding several terminations and substantive changes in local policing procedures.[12] How did Father Manship know to be at that location with a video camera? At IAF's National Training, with visible pastoral anger despite the passage of six years since these incidents and the subsequent campaign, he exclaimed, "They were beating the hell out my parishioners!" He knew this because he held ten to fifteen relational meetings each week in his large parish.

Father Manship's courageous leadership and highly relational ministry illustrate the obvious and powerful link between relational meetings and the mission of social change. This, alone, has the dynamic potential to inspire and embolden the church in one of its most significant practices mentioned previously: solidarity with the poor and marginalized. In other words, the church is relocated emotionally and geographically into vulnerable, marginalized, and often wounded spaces that make the church in practice what it was intended to be. The poor may always be with us, but doesn't this also imply that the church should be with the poor—that is, have some sense of what's going on in their lives and be invested in engaging with them to address the issues they face?

Clearly, a commitment to relational meetings is not just good pastoring and a catalyst to mission but also a profoundly theological action that relocates the church in both identity and action. Let's consider some of the other vital practices of the church that we used in the second chapter to discern "where" the church is or should be. Another of those practices was the "recognition of gifts," the belief that every person in a church has been spiritually endowed with a gift(s) that is essential to the life and mission of the body. The misshapen, unbiblical notion of a passive, consumptive, inarticulate, ungifted laity awaiting the direction of a wise, spectacularly gifted clergy dies entirely in this expectation. Recognizing the giftedness of all persons diversifies the body and its capabilities such that it functions in "the fullness of Christ." Relational meetings instantly become an essential and natural component of the social context in which these gifts are named and recognized.

Recall in the previous section we named assessing leadership capability as a primary goal of the meeting. In community organizing, this often means the ability to inspire and motivate others to action. Within the church, this concept of leadership is defined far more generously with a strong nod toward servanthood. Vital leadership, and the recognition of gifts precisely, defines all leadership as essential, and cannot occur when individual gifts are not publicly noticed or attributed. So often, relational meetings in the church setting can expand beyond the passions over injustices that drive persons to action (the staple of relational meetings in a community organizing context) to a level of personal and spiritual autobiography that reveals the deeper context of these passions. In this manner, we see another relocation of the church: being located in the passions, wounds, joys, stories, and giftings of every person in its community.

We also named the "rule of Christ," the commitment to live in a social politic of reconciliation by the persistent, humble, and prayerful extension of accountability (binding) and forgiveness (loosing) as a beautiful, challenging, and essential companion practice to the recognition of gifts. This "politics of forgiveness," as named by James McClendon, is a diligent process, a perpetual work of the church that is (or should be) constantly happening in multiple contexts and levels within a commitment to reconciliation. In our decades of ministry life, we have constantly witnessed how critical both relationship and story are to reconciliation. Animosity and division often diminish or even wither in the face of hearing the life stories and personal contexts of persons on the other side of struggle. Enemies can become co-laborers and even friends; this was surely the vision of Matthew's gospel (Mt. 5:43–44) that also provided the text for binding and loosing (Mt. 18:18) in a greater chapter on forgiveness. The relational meeting plays an obvious and vital role parallel to what McClendon called the "never-ending conversation" of reconciliation by building spiritual friendship, providing the intimate knowledge of common wounds and common vision, and intensifying the relational web of the community.

Living and working in reconciliation is a difficult challenge for every community, perhaps especially for churches and faith communities. By definition, these communities are points of social intersection for often our most intimate beliefs and greatest hopes or expectations. Such an intimate terrain inevitably involves conflict. In chapter six, we will discuss conflict very intentionally, making the counterintuitive point of its absolute necessity in the organizing church. The relational meeting and the listening session are absolutely essential antecedents and complements to the practice of the rule of Christ and a shared life of reconciliation in fellowships.

For specifically Christian congregations, constructing reconciling communities is uniquely challenging. Sadly, we not only reflect the deep divisions of our society, we also reinforce those divisions. Theologians such as Willie Jennings (currently at Yale Divinity School and formerly at Duke Divinity) have powerfully lamented that we baptize not only into a new creation but also into a church whose imagination has been damaged and "diseased" by a shameful racial and colonial heritage.[13] The Christian church being captured in a racial world of its own making is one of the most powerful explanations for the church's unwillingness to engage social change, since change inevitably indicts the church's own history. This is also, naturally, a dramatic barrier to the kind of spiritual transformation so deeply yearned for by so many pastors. Practices like the one-to-one relational meeting are a powerfully tangible way to release narratives that are silenced in our bureaucracies and our histories and then to generate real transformative action within and beyond our fellowships. The relational meeting helps relocate the church from spaces shaped by brokenness, division, and greed into a communal space driven by the work of reconciliation and sustained friendship.

In the next chapter, we will add the complementary practice to the relational meeting, the house meeting, or the listening session. This practice unleashes our stories in a communal setting with the force of directing the collective action of the community. Ultimately, it will amplify this most basic work of one-to-one relational meetings, the base and core of reorganizing the body of Christ.

5

RE-COLLECTING the Church: House Meetings and Discernment

When I (Dan) was in divinity school, I worked as an intern in a small, country Baptist church on the outskirts of Durham, North Carolina. It was a tight-knit community, with all the advantages and disadvantages of a small-town church. And like many young seminarians, I thought I had a pretty good idea of where they needed to grow and develop as disciples. I had a strong, self-assured sense of where the Spirit should lead them and how they might begin to really start living out the gospel. My agenda included a strong dose of social justice and, especially for this congregation, a "come to Jesus" altar call about the structural and generational realities of white rural racism.

My agenda was fairly obvious as I worked with the young people throughout the year, and many of the students were somewhat receptive to what I was trying to teach them. Still, I felt as if the church as a whole failed to recognize a latent racism they maintained. As is the case with the rest of culture, it lay just below the surface, affecting all aspects of the community, but was never overtly stated or seen. Sure that I was sent to be a prophet to this people, my time to confront them with the truth of this issue arrived as I was asked to preach a weeklong revival shortly after the end of my internship. My plan, as all camp speakers or revival preachers know, was to hit them with the call to repentance on evening three, having provided two prior days to build a relationship through funny jokes, intriguing stories, uplifting messages of God's love, and encouragement to meet the challenges they faced.

However, things rarely go according to plan, and I quickly found myself in quite an uncomfortable and awkward position. In an odd turn of events, a young woman from a Duke University athletics team I wanted to get to know had asked if she could come hear me preach. She was not a person of faith, but seemed interested in what I was doing. Many of you know how detrimental divinity school or seminary is to one's dating life, and though I was excited to have made it past the initial hurdle of exposing this career path, I knew this was a singularly bad idea. Not only was she coming on the wrong night and missing how charming and warm my prior messages had been, but, even more, she would lack the context to understand the deeper issues of this seemingly quaint congregation.

As you can imagine, the whole thing was a disaster. The sermon completely missed the congregation and, likely sounding more like a disorganized rant than a thoughtful, self-aware, and well-developed message, alienated the young woman as well. After exchanging a few awkward and curt e-mails, she never talked to me again.

It's not that this kind of prophetic message isn't desperately needed in our society and even embarrassingly tardy for our white communities. It's not that the gospel won't cost us mothers and fathers or sisters and brothers, let alone love interests. The issue in this instance was that my message originated from a position of distance and smug disinterest. I learned a lesson from this experience: a vision for change must also be matched with a mode of vulnerability, openness, attentiveness, and deep commitment to listening.

In my rush to correct and reprove the congregation regarding an issue of deep unfaithfulness that continues to plague much of our society, I'd failed to listen to them and to become deeply immersed in the struggles and challenges of their lives. I'd not taken the time to attend to the issues, desires, and stories within the congregation, failing to realize there were several longtime members who were deeply concerned about this issue and might have offered essential guidance for how we could begin to work on it as a community. Instead, I simply launched forward with a hard word of my own, lobbing critique and challenge from the sidelines like a bad coach criticizing players for failing to perfectly perform an ill-conceived game plan. The people of the community got in the way of my agenda for the church and what I thought I was supposed to do there.

* * *

To be honest, most of us as ministers and leaders have developed something of a natural allergy to listening. After all, we're constantly saturated with information from or about our congregations. Some of this information runs counter to our vision for the church or our theological understanding of what church should be or do. Other information includes externally offered ideals from church experts–such as growth specialists–or "suggestions" from within the congregation, both with thinly veiled disapproval of your passionate labor. Tuning out a bit or keeping a distance is often just a basic survival reflex. Too many sermon critiques, Sunday evening e-mails detailing issues, and late-night leadership meetings during which we've had our skills and vision evaluated have schooled us either to develop a tough shell or to become what Stanley Hauerwas and Will Willimon have described as a useless and exhausted "quivering mass[es] of availability."[1] And all this comes when the mission seems greater than ever, at the very time when our congregations are withering away and our outreach is truncated. There seems to be little time for listening in such an urgent situation. But listening, especially strategically organized listening, can be a great boon to both revitalization and learning how to faithfully follow the Spirit's lead.

Building with Open Ears

Originally one volume, the Old Testament books of Ezra and Nehemiah are about construction, or, better, *reconstruction.* They recount a story of mobilization, reconstitution, and renewal. As with all mobilization efforts, however, they are chock full of issues, setbacks, and confrontations. Their author is intent to keep these challenges before our eyes. Renewal and reconstruction constantly face the possibility of relapse, diversion, and hostile takeover. While some of these challenges emerge from external pressures and opposition, the most detrimental arise from internal strife: the momentum of fragmentation and disunity intrinsic to human community as a result of multiple interests and pursuits. We are quite familiar with the challenges Nehemiah encounters.

Nehemiah is not the initiator of this work; he's not even the first leader engaged in it. He's part of something that God began in the most shocking of ways, working through the Persian King Cyrus. Other leaders precede him in this intentionally theological

narrative: Zerubbabel, who leads the reconstruction of the temple
(Ezra 1–6), and Ezra, who leads the return of the people and the
reinstitution of the Law (Ezra 7–10). Nehemiah then sets about the
task of rebuilding the walls of the city of Jerusalem.[2] Thus, there's
a theological trajectory to this restoration project, moving from the
reconstruction of the temple to the return and reorganization of the
people to the physical rebuilding of the city's infrastructure, starting
with its walls. The end of exile and the renewal of the community
follow this pattern, moving from the center out.

But just as it is for us, the work is not so simple, straightforward,
or easy. As noted above, while the narrative recounts the events
of restoration, mobilization, return, and reinstatement, it also
includes episodes of relapse, moments of diversion, and constant
headaches and issues along the way that stall the efforts and even
at times hijack the work. Nonetheless, the book is meant to offer
hope and encouragement to communities involved in the work of
reconstruction, reiterating and validating their identity as the people
of God.[3] As Nehemiah discovers, renewing the community and
abiding in worshipful restoration requires addressing issues and
concerns of which he was unaware. He will have to lead by listening.

After some initial success in his venture to rebuild the city gates,
with the people unified in their work (Neh. 2:17–3:32), trouble starts
brewing. First, it comes from outsiders, "angry" and "enraged" by
this work and bent on stopping it (4:1–23). But soon Nehemiah
discovers that there is also *internal* strife flagging the work and
threatening to pull the community apart. There's something of a
pause button in the narrative at this point, as chapter five begins.
We are told "a great outcry" (v. 1) arose among the people over their
needs and the way their fellow kin were exploiting this opportunity
for gain. Echoing the "cry" of the people in Egypt (Ex. 2:23), this
uproar cannot be ignored, for the very dignity of the people and
integrity of the leadership are at stake. Recognizing the danger of
this situation and frustrated by it, Nehemiah calls the people together
in an "assembly" to do the community business of dealing with the
social crisis (Neh. 5:7).

Without falling prey to a crude moralization of this passage,
what's at stake here is not simply greed and usurious practices, but
ultimately what kind of people they will need to be to inhabit the
walls of this city, to live in this land, and to worship at the temple.
Mere reconstruction is not enough. To be restored as God's people
will require them to be a peculiar type of people, a community

that shares its goods in mutual provision instead of exploiting one another for gain, and wherein persons do not use their power to extort others. Nehemiah learns that to lead the people forward in their restoration, he will have to listen to discern how they can best become God's people.

What Nehemiah discovers here fits quite neatly with Paul's instruction on how to gather to do business in the Spirit, discussed in 1 Corinthians 14:23–33, and is depicted in the gathering of the church in Acts 15 to engage the young community's disagreement about the inclusion of the Gentiles. Furthermore, it fits soundly with the practice of the rule of Christ we outlined in chapter two. As Paul suggests, this process opens a space for anyone who feels led to take the floor and speak. Such open discussion also perceives that, because the healing work of Christ is not necessarily limited to the community, insight through dialogue may even come from beyond the congregation itself, so that they are not afraid to invite a wider circle of persons to speak at times–as with Abraham's encounter with Melchizedek (Gen. 14:18–20) or the Hebrews' interaction with Balaam (Num. 23–24).

As we have noted, church leadership requires the fostering of a continual conversation, an ongoing dialogue of perspectives on critical issues, for one cannot faithfully lead simply by talking all the time. To lead we must listen. Even in doing something as significant as rebuilding the walls, the internal character of the people must be sustained and renewed, a process fostered by privileging their cries and longings. Again, construction is not enough. In a post–*Field of Dreams* era, it's no longer clear that "if you build it, [they] will come"–or, more importantly, that if you build it, they will stay, or if you build it, they will be involved or will not destroy the entire community for their own gain. Walls and buildings, even budgets, don't make a people, particularly a people of God.

The Practice of House Meetings

Listening is a skill, and a collective style of listening requires a certain degree of technique and structure. To ensure that all are offered a chance to speak, that the cries of the community are registered, and that its desires and longings congeal in a certain direction compels us to look to proven practices for how to organize such activities. As a sister practice to the one-to-one relational meetings described in the last chapter, listening sessions (or house meetings, as we will sometimes call them) are a technique for gathering critical input, frustrations, desires, and hopes from the community. They are internal tools that help to initiate and forge deeper ties between people so as to consolidate them as a base on the edge of mobilization. Within listening sessions or house meetings, individual stories can congeal into community stories, and as they do, solidarity between individuals is cultivated. As experiences are heard, they echo and reverberate through the group, offering validation and amplification. At the same time, these experiences are refined and set within a larger context of other perspectives and experiences. As a result, not only do house meetings provide an instance for individual concerns and desires to be vocalized, but they also begin to congeal these interests in mutual understanding and into a collective pursuit.

Within the context of community organizing, organizers discovered the need to build off of their individual one-to-one meetings by bringing groups of people together to solidify connections and to amplify and legitimize hopes and concerns.[4] These kinds of house meetings were the backbone of the organizing of farmworkers begun by Fred Ross and championed by Cesar Chavez in the 1960s and 1970s. Gathering folks together after assuring them of what could be accomplished if they worked together, Chavez would invite the workers to share their stories, to describe the problems they faced, and express what they'd like to see happen. These hundreds of meetings formed the basic molecules of what came to be the United Farm Workers (UFW) union. As a practice now incorporated into organizing movements across the world, it has become a staple of the community organizing toolkit. Again, however, here–as with one-to-one meetings–it's a flexible technique or art, not a rigid formula. Let's define house meetings a bit more.

A house meeting is not a dinner club or a small group. Instead, it is a gathering of eight to twelve persons for the purpose of telling stories, identifying areas of mutual commitment and concern, and building shared identity through combining hopes, desires, frustrations, and possibilities for action. These are not weekly gatherings, but take place during intentional seasons of the community, as a way of co-creating an action agenda for the next few years. To this end, the meetings' goals are: (1) to build solidarity, (2) to identify shared concerns and interests, (3) to forge mutual vision around joint hopes, (4) to identify new leaders, and (5) to propose new action and discern possible ways forward. Further consolidating the relational fabric developed in individual meetings, in his study of community organizing, Jeffrey Stout observes, "[T]he house meeting retains the emotional contact of face-to-face interaction and the element of storytelling, but because it includes as many as a dozen people, it works somewhat differently and fulfills additional functions."[5] Within these meetings, people's individual stories, relayed in one-to-one meetings, strike resonances with others, and the vulnerability in sharing opens up the possibility of new connections. Serving to amplify the cries of those suffering wrongs and to discover overlapping themes, house meetings not only broaden connections within the organization but also begin to pave the way for mobilization—that is, for doing something together.

When leading a house meeting, the convener typically will begin by briefly articulating the reason for the gathering and then posing a few pointed but open-ended questions. Usually, these opening questions ask those gathered to share what brought them to the community and what they hope to see for its future. Again, as with the one-to-one meeting, some degree of agitation or pressing may be appropriate here in order to get people to voice their deeper passions, frustrations, and interests. It is not uncommon for folks to begin with more superficial or indirect answers, as many people are not comfortable speaking from a personal perspective or about deeply intimate issues. Agitation is not badgering or bullying, it's not being gruff or abrasive, but it's the art of inviting and gently pressing people to go a bit further than they are initially comfortable with going. Key to this is asking good follow-up questions, such as: "Why did you do that?" "Why is that meaningful to you?" or, "What makes that important to you?"

It's critical for you or a co-leader to take notes. These are not minutes of the meeting. Instead, you are chronicling the nature of the reasons for why people are there, what their connections to the community are, and what frustrations, passions, and desires are mentioned. Seasoned organizers have a sensitive ear for detecting stories that will resonate broadly, as well as for pinpointing recurrent themes, but these will not likely be evident to you until you review your notes with others. Having notes also is helpful for maintaining transparency, as you'll later want to collate and merge the data provided in these house meetings.

Finally, throughout the course of the house meeting, it's essential to look for leaders, or for those who seem to have a degree of energy or passion related to a specific issue or initiative. Indeed, it is the constant identification of leaders both in one-to-one meetings and in house meetings (and then the development of them) that most community organizers describe as the primary task of their work.

Sticking to the rules of organizing, a house meeting should typically last about an hour to an hour and a half, and it's important to be sure to start and end on time. Folks can always stick around longer if they choose (and they often do), but you'll find it easier to convene these meetings and recruit folks to lead them if you set a precedent for respecting everyone's time.

All of this holds true when using house meetings to help organize the church. As is already evident, beyond forging deeper relational ties, house meetings offer a significant and participatory mode of listening to the multiple voices of the community—something absolutely essential to the vitality of the church or any faith community. We describe our own process in more detail below, but one should already be able to see here how this process serves to build off of and bolster many of the basic social practices we described in chapter two that define the church. Again, it serves to generate solidarity between members and particularly allows for solidarity to develop with those whose voices might otherwise be marginalized or ignored. It also tends to reconnect the practice of the common table by intentionally naming real material needs and the concrete meaning of mutual provision in light of these needs.

House meetings provide a space for tangibly reaffirming baptismal vows and visions of the new creation. They offer another chance to recognize gifts and recover the fullness of Christ through the identification of new leaders, many of whom do not fit the typical "leader" profile. Lastly, they are invigorating for the practice of collective discernment and the politics of forgiveness. Challenges are acknowledged and visions for a process of moving forward are generated in this open space intentionally designated for these purposes. Fostering mutuality, house meetings not only alert the people to grievances or places we may be quenching the Spirit but also allow those frustrations to be vetted within an intimate gathering so as to begin to break members out of isolation and individualism and to invite shared wisdom through corporate discernment.

Who's Afraid of the Spirit's Lead?

We find it quite interesting that most pastors and churchgoers we talk to can recall a time of vibrancy in their community, a time when the Spirit was really moving. We also find it fairly telling that most of the time it is this very dynamic and somewhat uncontrollable life that so many of our congregations are structured to quell. As with any other institution, our churches seem often to default to the stable, the noncontroversial, and therefore the professional or hierarchical. Like our cultural overreliance on the pharmaceutical industry, we seem more satisfied managing the chronic condition of our churches than moving proactively toward greater health. We'd rather dictate than listen, finding it easier and less risky to set an agenda for the community than to open our authority to where the Spirit is leading amongst us. Lest you take us for naïve idealists on this point, both of us, as strong "J's" on the Myers-Briggs,[6] find this move toward chaordic listening quite challenging!

As a community, however, and particularly as leaders within a community, if we are going to be attentive to the life of the Spirit, we will have to become comfortable with being out of control. This is not to say that the Spirit can't work through top-down leadership, or that there's no place for church management or administration. However, it is also not too much to say that the Spirit's mode of leading is characteristically grassroots. For to be the church is to be a peculiar kind of institution that thrives in its vulnerability and openness to the leading of the Spirit, where we wait with open ears for what God is doing. Too often our communities become coopted by the whims of individual leaders. Too often these same individual leaders tend to coopt the community because they feel left on their own to lead, bearing all the responsibility for setting the course ahead. Through listening, then, we can begin to move in ways that are not agenda-driven, but invite collective discernment for the way to move forward. Embodying something closer to the *Gelassenheit* (or "open availability to the Spirit") of a Quaker meeting, with the tangibility, proximity, and intimacy of Wesleyan class meetings, and the mutual commitment and revolutionary potency of Catholic base communities, this mode of seeking consensus leans on the Spirit to lead in the context of the real circumstances of the community. Through such intentional listening, the work of our congregations is made consonant with the texture of who we actually are, such that the answer to the question, *Where is God leading us?* arises out of what's going on in the community. While certainly not something that must be done in every instance, this kind of listening practice can provide a way of rejoining a fragmented body, discovering festering wounds or places where its structure needs to be adjusted, and determining what new actions need to be taken or how to move forward faithfully together when the way is not clear.

This type of openness, interconnection, and vulnerable tending to one another, as our Jewish brothers and sisters in organizing have reminded us, can be understood to closely align with the Hebrew term ⌈*hesed.*⌉ While often rendered simply as loving-kindness, the term really encapsulates empathy, deep connection, and reciprocal understanding that moves from the inner core of each person to unite them with one another. Additionally, our Latino/a brothers and sisters in organizing have taught us to think of the deliberation and collective practical wisdom it leads to as an act of *averiguar,* a term whose meaning is derived from the two root words joined together to make it: *ver*–to see and *guar*–together. Thus, ⌈*averiguar*⌉ means to discuss, figure out, inquire, research, investigate, and discern or figure out together. As we've noted, for the church, it is exactly this activity or practice that invites the Spirit to lead, when we are willing to take the risk to engage in it.[7] For as Jesus says, "truly I tell you, if two of you agree on earth about anything you ask, it will be done for you by my Father in heaven. For where two or three are gathered in my name, I am there among them" (Mt. 18:19–20).

Listening Fosters Mutual Commitment and Mobilization

While it takes a certain amount of time and patience, we've found that making use of house meetings to listen and discern can have very practical results. We've even found that it can turn a real challenge into an opportunity for strengthening congregational commitment and kindling new energy, bringing forth new vitality around even the most basic of church housekeeping matters.

Our friend-mentor and longtime organizer with IAF, Gerald Taylor, tells a story about a black Lutheran congregation he worked with some years ago in the Queens borough of New York City. Like so many contemporary congregations, it was a struggling church formed from the merger of three failing congregations, and it had recently called a new minister. Having looked to the local community organization to help address an infestation of drug dealing on and around the church premises, with Gerald's help they'd been able to win a quick and decisive victory by garnering the help of the local police. This victory boosted their ego a bit and established some recognition in the community. Shortly afterward, however, they were mired in a stewardship campaign that was failing miserably, with very few of the members actually signing pledges. Again, the minister turned to Gerald for some help.

At that point, Gerald asked the pastor and church leadership if they'd asked the people what their priorities for the community were. Essentially, he wanted to know, had they engaged in listening to the needs, desires, cries, and priorities of the members? Brushing this question off, the pastor and leadership relayed that they already knew what the priorities of the community were, so there was no need to engage in this activity. Always one for a good challenge (and quick to see a savvy opportunity, we would add), Gerald suggested that they "make a deal." He proposed that they let him run a series of house meetings to elicit the priorities of the community and then draw up their capital campaign based on those concerns. Then, if any of the priorities matched their pre-named priorities or they didn't make budget, he'd cut their dues to IAF in half. On the other hand, if a new set of priorities emerged and they made budget, then they would agree to double their dues to the organization. You can likely guess the conclusion. At the end of the series of house meetings, not a single priority pre-identified by the church leadership made the list. Even more, when the church redesigned the campaign around the priorities that emerged from the house meetings (getting a new heating system and new carpet for the sanctuary, establishing some Bible study training), 147 out of 150 members made pledges, allowing them to raise their entire budget—with a surplus, to boot. Of course, Gerald called in his side of the deal, and this congregation went on to become the fastest-growing and largest black Lutheran church in New York City: New Hope Lutheran Church.

Our own experience in conducting house meetings has proved vital for reinvigorating and mobilizing our community as well. About five years ago, we initiated a season of house meetings in our congregation, believing that as a community we were struggling with some conflicting aspirations among our leadership and the accompanying confusion among the body. Having become more comfortable after the space move we described in the previous chapter, which had resulted in the conclusion of a few ministry initiatives correlated with our prior location, and having had some turnover in our congregation, there was a sense that the community's vitality was running a bit low, or at least had plateaued. New folks were not exactly sure how to get involved, even as some of our leaders had moved on. So, we recruited a handful of people we knew would be willing to host house meetings and would be able to round up eight to twelve others for a more intentional time of listening and discussion. We also specified that they seek out people who were not in their immediate friend group or small group (if they had one). Then, we asked that they conduct these meetings within a determined timeframe with the idea that we would all gather together after this period to bring our notes together, to collate them, and to see what we found. The results were both invigorating and surprising.

Coming together, our leaders took turns relaying their notes and transferring them to large white post-it pages. Once each leader finished, we hung their notes on the wall, eventually encircling the room. What became visibly evident from doing this were converging themes and concerns, two of which subsequently became significant missional initiatives in the life of our community. The first of these was a desire to work more intentionally with ex-offenders as part of a larger approach to engage the issue of violence and mass incarceration in our city. Hence, we formed a new ministry partnership with an organization that creates "faith teams" to assist local citizens transitioning from incarceration. The second was an interest in reaching out more to refugees being settled in our area, which yielded another vibrant and meaningful ministry partnership. The deep effects of these two initiatives on our community cannot be overstated.

Both brought a new level of energy to the congregation in areas that grew the edges of our community while incorporating new leaders and people into active engagement. Additionally, these new leaders were able to exercise particular gifts of hospitality, patience, compassion, friendship, and service fitting for these very tasks that would have never had the opportunity for expression without them. Both initiatives also profoundly shaped our identity. For instance, as our faith team began to accompany a certain ex-offender, he began to attend our community—engaging in the sermon dialogue and breaking bread with us at the table. He eventually brought other friends who have become equally beloved persons in the church. We truly are not the same, and the buzz of the new vitality can be tangibly felt in the weekly gathering.

The long-term impacts were even greater. Our faith team's new missional partnership with the Religious Coalition for a Non-Violent Durham (led by the truly remarkable Marcia Owen) has continued to draw us into new depths of understanding and action related to how violence and mass incarceration shape our city and our nation.[8] This organization holds a community vigil to memorialize every life lost to violence in Durham. We have helped lead these memorials, and our congregation regularly attends them. For Advent, we have crafted a liturgical tradition wherein we name each of these lost neighbors. We are also raising money to buy gravestones for the parents of those lost who fear they have not only lost their children but have no way to remember them or mark their existence because they can't afford a marker. And quite dramatically, when two local organizations, the Southern Coalition for Social Justice (SCSJ) and Fostering Alternatives to Drug Enforcement (FADE) approached Durham CAN with alarming statistics about racialized policing in Durham, we were ready to help lead a broad-based action that resulted in the development of a monumental policy change toward written consent for all vehicle searches by police in Durham, the validation by the local police of IDs issued by their faith communities (Faith IDs) for our immigrant population, the cessation of "faith community checkpoints" (intentional police surveillance at faith communities with high Latino/a attendance during worship services), the termination of the Durham Police Chief, and a citywide commitment for a culture change to community policing. I (Tim) had the privilege to help lead Durham CAN's work on these initiatives with a highly engaged congregation supporting every meeting, assembly, confrontation, and step of this process.

Of course, we are by no means perfect. Our house meeting process, though immensely transformative to Emmaus Way, did not work perfectly either. In fact, you should expect to encounter challenges. Some folks will be disgruntled with the process. For us, a small but beloved group of our congregation was upset when not everything they had suggested in their house meeting was implemented in the weekly gathering, particularly with regard to the liturgy and our collective worship. There were many tough conversations as a result, and surely misunderstanding on both sides. Some of this, no doubt, could be attributed to the fact that we could have run the process better and been more organized. But as we recognized, and as we hope you'll keep in mind, in a culture so steeped in independence and products aimed at giving us what we want, it takes time to train people into collaboration, compromise, and consensus-building. In a "have-it-your-way" culture, the collective house meeting process of priority-setting can be quite difficult. One friend of ours for many years (well before the founding of our church) eventually left our community, explaining that the process invoked a hopefulness in her that the community would take a new direction. But when the community ultimately didn't embrace this preferred direction, she became dismayed and disappointed, prompting her to leave. Though extremely painful at times—and losing this community member and her family was so—it was crucial to allow the collective discernment of the house meeting process to set the direction and focus of the community and galvanize our congregation in moving ahead.

Our community, having been introduced to the process, was then more prepared to embrace and enact our next season of listening. When Dan moved to Chicago two years ago (and we had another beloved staff member nearing the completion of his dissertation), we knew that we would inevitably need to reshape our staff. Anticipating these changes, our new lay leaders and the leadership team suggested another round of house meetings, a suggestion greeted with genuine enthusiasm by the community. Our lay leaders and our staff team leader and facilitator, Ben Haas, did an amazing job leading us in priority-setting and developing four initiative areas. Here is Ben's summary of one vital community commitment on "Diversity and Substance":

> We value the diversity and substance of our community dialogue (e.g., relationships, theology, the arts).
>
> We long to further embrace and expand our community's diversity. That includes a desire to seek out/accommodate new voices and a desire to create more diverse ways of engaging our community.
>
> We would like our community to be a space that interrupts our cultural captivity and draws us into countercultural practices in our social, economic, and relational lives.

This commitment has yielded many dividends. We intentionally hired Molly (mentioned earlier) from outside our existing community network. She has been an amazing co-pastor in Dan's absence. She has already diversified our community with new theological passions and with new congregants from her friendship circle who have become exciting new voices in our dialogue.

In addition, while already a radically inclusive community that practices an open Eucharist table each week, we heard in this second round of house meetings that we needed to be more intentional in both naming and advertising our existing enthusiasm to gracefully receive LGBTQ persons. We had become painfully aware how much risk is involved for the queer community to discern churches that are safe to attend. Our commitment to hospitality would certainly require that we minimize that fear. I (Tim) had so much enthusiasm for this direction, I fear I overreached initially and short-circuited the process in defining how we would proceed. Despite the general consensus about pursuing a more vocal hospitality, several folks were frustrated that they could not be more involved with how it would happen. Nevertheless, cleaning up my impatience produced several significant relational meetings that, as always, deepened relationship in the community. As this illustrates, there is an intimate, ongoing interconnection between relational meetings and house meetings such that they support each other in the formation of a healthy, resilient, and thick community.

We are reminded in the gospel of John (3:8) that the Spirit remains untamable, prone to movement beyond our control-addicted lives, outrunning the confines constructed for her. She does not follow us, but, rather, we must learn to attend to and listen for her moving, letting her lead us. Such is the life of the church—or the church as it should be. Communities more equipped to listen and more dedicated to this practice through the process of listening sessions and house meetings will also become more active and dynamic—that is, more like the Spirit they seek to follow. Such active and vibrant congregations, however, will inevitably encounter conflict, for often it is their very active nature that provokes conflict. But as we will see in the next chapter, if we are not to quench the Spirit, but to continue to embody her life, embracing the presence of Christ and following in his path, then we will also have to learn how to engage conflict in light of the gospel—that is to say, to engage it in a constructive manner that can actually enliven and strengthen the community rather than drag it down or destroy it. To go forward, therefore, we must address the role of conflict.

6

RE-UNITING the Church:
On Conflict and Revitalization

To be honest, ministry is often boring. When it's not boring, it's often painful. Caught between maintaining the status quo and death by a million cutting comments, it rarely seems active or adventuresome. Weeks tend to be consumed with meetings—that is, when they're not pushed aside so we can put out the most recent fire or fend off attacks. Is it any wonder that so many leaders in ministry are anxious, depressed, and lonely?

If we admit it, most of us have been disciplined to avoid action. Those of us who didn't figure it out quickly have likely learned the hard lesson of just how turbulent life in ministry can be when you try to prod the herd. And we've got the scars to prove it! One of our favorite church leadership cartoons captures this reality perfectly.

"We're hoping you'll lead us on a journey of transformation without requiring any real changes."

78

More than one ministry has been broken to pieces by the ire and resentment provoked by attempted change, even when people have asked for it. Even more ministries have succumbed to the gradual captivity of bureaucracy, simply happy to avoid the destruction active change might bring. As a result, many of our congregations simply become demobilized, falling into maintenance mode organizations or fragmenting into apathetic indifference. To develop healthy and active congregations—and we will suggest that there is no way around this—our congregations have to learn to engage conflict. As any organizer worth his or her salt knows, action creates friction, and no movement is possible without it. Thus, in this chapter, we contend that too often as leaders, in our efforts to avoid conflict, we end up creating congregations that are fixated on maintenance or captive to centralized control rather than active involvement. Hence, we argue that a component essential to rehabilitating and reinvigorating our congregations is the somewhat counterintuitive practice of learning to engage conflicts.

We recognize just how treacherous this territory is, especially given the state of the church these days. We do not mean to be Pollyanna-ish or naïve on this point. In all reality, given our greater social context, there is much to fight about, and conflict seems to be everywhere. The future of our communities feels precarious. We live in a time of significant change and pervasive uncertainty. And despite the sense that we probably know more now than we as a society ever have, or at least have more information at our finger tips, the world we find ourselves in seems to be getting only more complex, divided, and unknowable. A global world seems to be both smaller than ever due to communications and travel, and yet, at the same time, it also seems to be much larger when we start to consider the multiplicity of issues plaguing it. Diverse, contesting, and even hybrid perspectives compete in a context of pluralism, leaving many of us bewildered and, if we're truthful, scared. On a daily basis we are confronted with political entrenchments, especially in the era of the never-ending election cycle and entertainment-politics. Economic disparities, unemployment, lack of opportunity, crime, social isolation, and divisions along the lines of race, gender, sexuality, and age persist. Between the "clash of civilizations" and the "culture wars," real conflicts and disagreements seem certain to only perpetuate global instability and social fragmentation.[1] The issues run deep; they're complex, and at times seem to be beyond our capacity to engage. Add to this context the interpersonal skirmishes that dog every human community, and it's no wonder we often feel so stuck, so defeated, and so paralyzed. Even the most optimistic commentators must admit that the future we face is a bit unknown; we're not entirely sure how to go forward even as we realize there's a lot at stake and a lot to be done.

With all the uncertainty, frustration, and wounding that accompanies conflict, it's easy to see why most of our congregations trend toward centralized control or maintenance modes of operation. It's not surprising many of us try to avoid conflict at all costs or stamp it out immediately, even when this directly deactivates our congregations. In attempting to avoid or eradicate conflict, however, we unintentionally also keep our congregations from becoming active and vibrant. While this should not be confused with celebrating conflict or encouraging it, learning to engage conflict well can be a unique opportunity for building healthier and stronger relationships within the community, as well as for developing the skill of collective discernment so desperately needed within our communities if we are going to faithfully move forward. We've come to realize, through experience in community organizing, that the practice of wholesomely engaging conflict also rests on a deep, if often ignored, theological principle for how to address wrongs and make decisions in light of the gospel. Relying on skills learned through community organizing and theological precepts derived from the ecclesial practice of the rule of Christ, described in chapter two, we contend that, as weird as it may sound, engaging conflict can be both enlightening and galvanizing for your community.

Before describing the healthy process of engaging conflict and its benefits for your community, however, we want to first describe common ways congregational leaders evade conflict and how these strategies tend to contribute to the demobilization and constriction of our communities. These examples of avoiding conflict and the organizational structures they facilitate will provide a sharp and informative relief to the practices we will eventually recommend in this chapter.

Evasion and Deactivation

Let's admit it up front: we're all afraid of conflict. This fear is warranted and even wise, as a certain level of fear distinguishes the brave from the foolhardy. But it can also overly determine how we attempt to deal with conflict. Through years of observation and dialogue with pastors, we have found there are several common strategies pastors and churches deploy to avoid or stamp out conflict, each with potentially crippling and debilitating consequences for the body. The short list that follows is not exhaustive. Nevertheless, many readers will recognize these approaches. Before launching into the list, we confess we have been uniquely skilled evaders of conflict. At times we have been so skilled at avoidance that we have artfully combined several of these strategies in the same context. We've also seen our community flag in vitality as a result. We write as the guilty, to the guilty, with an earnest desire to courageously pursue alternative approaches.

Evasion by Tolerance

The first evasive approach arises from what might be called the sacred virtue of contemporary, middle-class American culture: tolerance. As an approach that occurs commonly in many different churches, its basis rests in an implicit bias for what sociologist Alan Wolfe has called "capacious individualism" run through a framework of politeness.[2] A stance so ingrained in our popular consciousness it hardly needs explanation, capacious individualism takes the perspective that "you can do what you want, so long as you let me do what I want," with the added caveat that we don't intentionally hurt anyone. As the foundation for an approach to conflict, the strategy usually acknowledges the existence of difference or division, but politely (and "respectfully") steers clear of confrontation and the messiness of contestation and its accompanying pain or angst. Privileging what they might term as decorum or proper etiquette to the disturbance of conflict, many congregations make it a practice simply not to talk about controversial issues or places of significant disagreement.[3] Through the acceptance of tolerance, congregations employing this approach generally tend to live most predominantly by our larger culture's eleventh commandment: "Thou shalt not judge."[4]

As theologian and social critic David Hollenbach, S.J., notes, however, tolerance as acceptance is "entirely inadequate" to deal with many of the problems and issues that divide us.[5] It's hard to imagine the practice of tolerance could resolve issues of urban poverty, institutional racism, sexism, budget crises, abuse, or social isolation, let alone foster active dedication needed for strong and healthy communities. The tolerant body here seems to lack a healthy immune system, and as a result tends to keep a low-grade infection, as underlying disputes, differences, and divisions inhibit its vitality, deleteriously affecting its energy level, active engagement in mission, and long-term health.

The most obvious effect of the feebleness of tolerance is demobilization. Gerald Taylor, our friend and mentor mentioned earlier, speaks unyieldingly about this situation. Taylor is a veteran of some of the most difficult struggles for justice, including the fight for civil rights and intense local battles for educational equity, affordable housing, and living wages in New York, Baltimore, Memphis, Atlanta, and North Carolina. On numerous occasions, we have seen Taylor prepping a group of clergy and other faith-based leaders for social/ political action only to have some individual ask whether there is a nicer or more "mannered" way to engage. Someone inevitably states a version of, "Do we have to be so rude or abrasive?" to which he unflinchingly retorts, "You can't expect this type of change without a fight." Recognizing the frequent correlation between this posture and general privilege, he then often follows up on this remark by saying, "We are never going to get anything done around here because we have too many nice, white liberals in the room!" This should not be mistaken for brute hyper-masculinity, though certainly at times organizing has taken this tone. Taylor's point is that social justice and real change rarely, if ever, occur without the intentional confrontation of the Powers that benefit from injustice and want to maintain the status quo. Action necessitates friction.

Too many churches allow the threat of discomfort to overly determine their engagement. The result tends to be a diminished or stale body that, while wishful in its talk, struggles to embody the transformative movement of the gospel. We certainly don't mean to downplay the importance of tolerance in a pluralist context. But we also want to acknowledge that churches shaped most centrally by this value suffer from an inability to foster the real intimacy and active missional engagement required by the vision of the gospel.

Evasion by Intolerance

If tolerance as acceptance is one widely practiced way churches attempt to evade conflict, then the flip side of tolerance–intolerance–may be just as profuse. Typically, it's an approach to conflict that occurs in congregations and communities dominated by authoritarian/charismatic figures. These often phenomenally skilled people, employing the varying guises of CEO, hipster, apostolic genius, or spiritual guru, tend to hold discursive and ideological sway over the souls of their communities. In many large churches, this dominance is by intentional design. The theology, management style, and politics of the head figure are promulgated as the theology, structure, and politics of the community under the implication that this is the *only* way to do or see things. His or her (but usually his) way of thinking, preferred clichés or terms, and even personality become idealized and held up for adoration and imitation by the community, monopolizing the community's identity, mission, and overriding vision. The leader's tone of discourse, whether generous, whimsical, absolute, or even profane, becomes the norm of community speech. As a mark of strong leadership, decisiveness, and vision, this central leader tolerates no questioning or disagreement, often flexing his muscle to weed out or suppress any contrary voice or position. It's his way or the highway.

Anyone who has experienced the frustration associated with having to attend meeting after meeting as part of a bureaucratic process that seems only to come to a decision once it's too late can understand why leaders might function this way. A central decision maker offers the attraction of efficiency and clear direction. Sadly, in our experience, the single-minded confidence of leadership often becomes hard to distinguish from the arrogance that cloaks insecurity or the lack of humility that accompanies overconfidence. Too often, strong leadership comes to mean the leader always getting his way, and an unwavering resistance to considering other perspectives or listening to opposing suggestions. Under this type of congregational leadership, disagreement is unacceptable. One's ability to immediately quash opposition or rout any challenge often becomes the mark of good and solid administration. Frequently over-masculinized in its expression, figures operating in this mode don't so much avoid conflict as disallow it, creating a culture where leadership means aggressively calling all the shots and dispelling any dissenters. It's not hard to imagine the losses intrinsic to the approach, even if you haven't had to experience it personally.

Indeed, the losses here are large. The gospel becomes reductive to the preferences, styles, and perspective of a single, unchallenged pastoral icon. Because conflict is perceived as a threat to his or her leadership and vision, the dominant leader suppresses it or moves rapidly to excise anyone who has a differing perspective. As a result, the healthy diversity of perspectives (and there's always more diversity in a congregation than may be visible on the surface) is squelched and, along with them, genuine possibilities for new knowledge, creative alternatives, and the mutual commitment derived from deliberating together. The flip side of the church of tolerance, the body here becomes captive to an overly aggressive immune system that begins to attack its own organs, leaving it constantly set against itself and incapable of functioning holistically.

Some sense of unity may be present, but it tends to be forged in coercion or through the deactivation of its own members. Community discussions get thinned out, and relationships become homogeneous, leaving them trivial and superficial. At the same time, it engenders a culture of fear and protectionism that usually results in constriction and eventual suffocation. When fear and protectionism dominate under such a strong personality, the congregation loses its ability to discern together what it means to be faithful when it faces new circumstances or encounters challenges. An inverse relationship develops between the growing power of the central leader and the declining capacity for rich involvement from the community. Absent are the deep struggles and reconciliations of intimate communities addressing the complexities of life. The faculty of collective wisdom never gets developed, and learning is stifled. Consequently, the congregation fails to mature as a result of wrestling with real and unresolved issues, and its understanding and practice of the gospel is debilitated.

Evasion by Hopeful Avoidance

In this final strategy, I (Tim) will part ways with Dan. This is my favorite conflict avoidance scheme. Often, I tend to impart too much of what I *hope* will happen to those engaged in conflict. My position as pastor certainly does not help. In this role, I am usually ministering to people on both sides of a dispute, and I always try to do so with pastoral sensitivity and care. My job requires that I step back and try to see the best possibility for persons in my care. At times I've realized, however, this can mean seeing a different version of them than the one present, something I don't always acknowledge or communicate completely. Additionally, by nature I'm inclined to envision instances with a certain pastoral wishfulness, believing that the best might inevitably occur. These tendencies can downplay the causes or possible consequences of struggle. The problem for the body is that this approach tends to be like attempting to "walk off" a fractured leg. Not only does the leg get worse, it slowly tends to overwork or even damage other parts of the body as they try to compensate.

In the early days of Emmaus Way, similar to a lot of new organizations, we attracted many strong individualists–gifted persons who liked the possibilities of personal expression and the absence of bureaucratic limitations that a small, fledgling congregation provided. Initially, as a smaller group oriented by a creative but unrealized vision, there was little conflict. There was room for everyone to operate in his or her own preferred manner without really bumping into each other. As our community grew in numbers and developed deeper and more integrated relational connections, however, some of these freedoms disappeared. Eventually, no area of responsibility could operate on its own island, and some friction began to develop around different artistic, aesthetic, and procedural preferences. At this time, I was both enchanted by the vision that was emerging and engaged pastorally with many of the early leaders who came to the community with great gifts and, sometimes, deep relational wounds. As a result, I regularly ignored or downplayed how actions born of unrealistic expectations or personal pain rippled throughout the community, causing frustration and increasing division.

Dan, who is not prone to commit this type of wishful avoidance, had come to our community and joined the staff about a year before this season of struggle began. Thankfully, he had gathered his voice quickly enough to speak urgently about this situation in our collective lives. In less abrupt terms, he challenged me with the fact that I was unintentionally letting a few issues and some persons under my care hold the community hostage to their wounds or preferences. As I began to ask around, I found that his challenge was perhaps offered more gently than the circumstance demanded. People were not attending or were disengaging in certain areas because of the intransigence of key leaders. My avoidance strategy was unknowingly engendering detachment in a community intentionally founded on dialogue, collaborative worship, and shared action. In other words, our divisions, though rooted in some missional instincts and the real needs of our people, were actually beginning to threaten our community's identity and mission. My hopeful avoidance was merely letting a hairline fracture grow, allowing more serious and widespread rupture and decay to set in.

Evasion and Letting Bullies Win

We want to conclude this list with a short comment on bullies. Every type of community has bullies, and doubtless a room of ministers could trade stories for hours about the ones in their congregations. Many of these bullies can be absolutely charming in certain contexts and, indeed, usually do have a genuine faith and can exude strong leadership qualities. Nevertheless, a conflict-avoidant environment can offer tremendous license to these characters, inevitably producing a climate of trepidation, self-protection, diminished prophetic voices, or passivity. Whether intentionally or not, they take a community hostage, exhausting and persistently overwhelming challengers and bystanders alike. They often conceive of themselves as "staff managers," usually calculating a running tab of the staff's hours based solely on their knowledge of what's going on. For example, they write critical e-mail essays on Monday mornings, evaluating the Sunday worship service and pointing out every flaw. They believe their financial contributions, social status, or plain good looks entitle them to significant benefits or rights within the fellowship. In an argument or confrontation about scripture, they always have an original language translation that supports their perspective or offer credentials that they believe give them the high ground.

You know these parishioners or pastors; their favorite texts or scholars can always beat up yours. God is always in their corner. And heaven forbid when these persons get book contracts, have popular blogs, or have unique skills to support their dominance! Shutting down conversation and reflection, they remain intent on conforming the community to their mold. They win, but everyone else loses. As mentioned above, the costs can be extreme. Indifference and apathy, or sheer exhaustion, replace discipleship, the cultivation of leadership, or the pursuit of mission in realms guarded by bullies. Maturation and action are stunted. When bullies dominate, leadership is reduced to self-preservation, appeasement, or triage, and the greater capacities of the community are truncated. Mobilization is undermined, and, as is all too familiar, the community's life tends to degenerate under such a threat.

Conflict and the Edge of the Gospel

When we evade conflict, our congregations tend to devolve and become demobilized. Relational health, corporate vitality, and missional impact all suffer. Additionally, our ability to know how to resolve conflict, discern together, or make decisions atrophies or never develops. On the one hand, the relational fabric of the community never is tightly knit in the unique way that working through issues together makes possible, as any healthy family would attest. On the other hand, active engagement is thwarted. In the end, our congregations fail to learn how to achieve real, healthy resolution involving forgiveness, reconciliation, and transformation. Even more, the witness and service that make up the content of the church's mission become distorted, greatly curtailed, or completely inactive.

Jesus was no stranger to conflict. After all, as our gospels attest, his active mission eventually got him executed for being a political troublemaker. Jesus, however, was not simply controversial for the sake of being controversial or drawing attention to himself. Similarly, his active mission was not a competitive drive to establish his brand. He did not initiate conflicts in order to promote his celebrity or increase book sales. But Jesus was controversial, and his followers were active instigators. (Think of the book of Acts, for instance!) Many of our churches today, however, are either dying a slow, bourgeois death of bureaucratic management or succumbing to the distortion of personality cultism. Instead of action, we have meetings, promote officers, stress programs, write endless reports, and continue to create groups whose permanence is presumed. Instead of real discussions and deliberations, we look for someone to give us the answers or to tell us what to do. Our congregational brands become bigger and bigger, as the real depth and scale of our work becomes smaller.

The gospel Jesus preached and embodied, however, was inherently conflictual. How else could one read his bold and perhaps enigmatic statement, "Do not think that I have come to bring peace to the earth; I have not come to bring peace, but a sword" (Mt. 10:34)? Or, again, "I came to bring fire to the earth... Do you think I have come to bring peace to the earth? No, I tell you, but rather division!" (Lk. 12: 49a, 51). Yikes! It would appear that Jesus clearly recognized that the mission of his life would create conflict, that the decisive act of God in him would generate controversy, disagreement, and even clashes. A church awash in a society of individualist consumerism such as ours can easily slide into preaching a gospel that has lost its edge in our attempt to be relevant or to minister in this context. That the *Missio Dei* could be an action in contrast to our way of doing things, our security, or our right to the pursuit of happiness can seem foreign.

And the challenge of this active mission would not confront only those on the "outside." Even more, Jesus knew his followers, the "insiders," would continue to have conflicts amongst themselves, recognizing that living within the dynamism of this gospel path would not exactly be easy and would, therefore, require continued accountability and forgiveness (Mt. 18). In fact, we get the idea that participating in this transformative action of God would require constant transformation and reform within (*"Ecclesia semper reformanda est!"* [The church is to be always reforming], as theologian Karl Barth said). To live in communion with the living God set on restoring God's creation cannot be easy or static.

It's a bit hard to imagine in our society, in which Jesus and a static notion of the church typically stand for conservatism and the status quo, but in Jesus' day and for the early followers of "the way," his cause was quite disruptive. In Luke's account, Jesus' ministry establishes and enacts nothing short of jubilee, a practice so radical that, although written into the Israelite law, seems never to have been performed. The jubilee required the leveling of every gain achieved at the expense of others (land gains or human servitude) every fiftieth year, and was designed to specifically prevent the formation of a permanent, multigenerational impoverished class in Israel. This is left of left—the kind of call for prophetic action that seems so outrageous it's surely meant simply to be provocative. And yet, Jesus launches his ministry with a radical text from Isaiah declaring just such a jubilee:

> "The Spirit of the Lord is upon me,
>   because he has anointed me
>   to bring good news to the poor.
> He has sent me to proclaim release to the captives
>   and recovery of sight to the blind,
>   to let the oppressed go free,
> to proclaim the year of the Lord's favor." (Lk. 4:18–19)

Then, to the agitation of all in earshot, he goes on to claim that this event is fulfilled in his coming. It's a shocking pronouncement, but one nonetheless foreshadowed in his mother's song of glee upon receiving news from the angel of coming birth:

> "He has shown strength with his arm;
>   he has scattered the proud in the thoughts of their
>   hearts.
> He has brought down the powerful from their thrones,
>   and lifted up the lowly;
> he has filled the hungry with good things,
>   and sent the rich away empty" (Lk. 1:51–53).

Such actions and statements today would certainly be scorned as rabble-rousing or class warfare!

Similarly, it was not teaching the virtues of civil religion that got Stephen stoned, Paul and Silas beaten and imprisoned in Philippi, or John exiled to Patmos. It wasn't their devotion to the *status quo* for which early Christians drew the wrath of Rome. Indeed, they were persecuted for being "haters of God and humanity" and accused of being seditionists! But it's also clear from the New Testament witness, as well as early church history, that the church itself was often in disagreement about what it meant to follow Jesus. From the very beginning, the community realized that it would need to discern together what it would mean to participate in this decisive work of God, as there wasn't a definitive manual for how to go forward. The transformative nature of the gospel path would challenge those who had much to lose, just as its call would also require everything–even from those who had nothing. Clearly, the early communities struggled to figure out exactly what it meant to embody this message, things were not all settled, folks were not always on the same page, and at times they were even quite a mess–as many passages attest (Acts 15, 1 Corinthians, Galatians). Active change inherently involves struggle, negotiation, confrontation, unvarnished honesty, risk and failure, and vulnerability that are all part of collective discernment. To be a church on the move, a "church militant" in the true sense of the term, implies that this action and movement will at times generate conflict and disagreement. That much we can count on.

If the way forward for the church is to continue to move into the restorative mission of God, following in the path of Jesus and the testimony of scripture, then it seems this will require passing through conflicts or at least learning how to deal with them and learn from them. We believe this is true. Siding with the many visionaries and laborers who have called for community life organized by the practices of forgiveness and reconciliation, we want to propose that this path of faithful discernment can only be worked out through the processes of agitation, confrontation, and dialogue, rather than the wider path of conflict avoidance.

Rules for Radicals, and the Rule of Christ

Conflict is an intrinsic part of human society. Anyone who thinks otherwise is not being realistic. However, this does not mean we have to remain subject to conflict, or that there is no way forward through disagreements or competing power claims. That's just as unrealistic, if not theologically suspect, as we'll point out later. In his organizing textbook, *Rules for Radicals,* Saul Alinsky points to the inevitability of conflict as a part of the work for change. The central role of conflict was an insight Alinsky reached early on that gave shape to his own style of organizing. As he states, "Conflict is the essential core of a free and open society. If one were to project the democratic way of life in the form of a musical score, its major theme would be the harmony of dissonance."[6] This is another one of the elements that often scares so many church-folk away from organizing. However, organizers learn from the beginning that much of their work will require them to move into conflict, as opposed to running from it or quashing it automatically. After all, it's through conflict that most of what they are trying to do gets done. Building strong and lasting relationships and fostering transformation are not easy, for in any community there are always competing pressures that attempt to tilt things toward their own interest. As Alinsky reminds us, "Change means movement. Movement means friction."[7] To the extent that things are constantly changing around us and there are things around us that we want to change, friction naturally builds up as a result of this movement. But friction need not mean breakdown or immobility, for when channeled into the proper procedure, it can also contribute vital heat to the building of stronger relations and more just and peaceful arrangements. While community organizers are profoundly realistic, they are no less radical.

Recognizing the place of conflict, organizing at times and in certain instances actually encourages it through the practice of agitation. Agitation is not pestering, exasperating, or simply annoying someone. Instead, it is the practice of prodding a person or a group in order to bring issues to a head, to surface and even intensify them in order to call forth honesty and the gravity of the division. It serves to sharpen one's sense of a wrong being done to them, to clarify lines of discord, or to intensify the tension between things as they are and things as they should be. Agitation is necessarily present in effective relational meetings and listening sessions, whether by getting an individual to express a passion held close to the vest in a one-to-one, or exposing currents of need or desire in a house meeting. At times, agitation may push to exaggerate these divisions or disagreements as a means of bringing them out more fully. At this point, the nice Christians usually begin to turn away, opting for one of the strategies of avoidance so as not to stir the nest or make anyone mad at them. After all, as Dennis Jacobsen notes, "Agitation is impolite."[8] But as an integral part of accountability, organizers know that agitation and conflict are important for cultivating mutual recognition and collective commitment.

While the place of conflict and the tactics of agitation, listening and dialogue, generating tension, and working for resolutions within community organizing comprise and are contained within the practice of democratic politics, our engagement with these activities and practice of them have led us to return to some basic theological insights on the role of engaging conflict within the church community. In fact, relying on the practice of the rule of Christ (or "binding and loosing") we discussed in chapter two, we have come to see the critical role that engaging conflict plays within the life, mission, and identity of the church. Indeed, we have found that, far from conflict being something that is always and only degenerative for the life and mission of a congregation, engaging it in the right way might actually be at the heart of what the church is called to be and to do. As we have suggested, *it is in this practice that the church discovers the power and leading of the Spirit for building strong and healthy relationships, enacting the full scope of its mission, and obtaining wisdom for how to move forward.*

As a practice of endless conversation and forgiveness, the rule of Christ provides a real community process for engaging conflict and making practical judgments about how the community should proceed together. It's essential to the life of an active and vibrant congregation, not only for getting back on track when wrongs or issues develop within, but also because it promotes the kind of open deliberation in the power of the Spirit that allows the community to entertain new information or new circumstances, reconsider its practices and structures, discover new possibilities, and harmonize itself in unity to make decisions. In doing so, deeper solidarity is forged and active involvement is encouraged.

The rule of Christ integrates powerfully within the framework of the relational culture of the community (covered in chapter four); agitation and tension can play a role in building solidarity and clarifying concerns. It's important to be clear here, because this can easily appear to provide license to leaders who thrive on division or are looking for justification to be rude or obnoxious. Agitation is not abuse, and creating tension is not terrorizing. Instead, these are techniques that attempt to push past the circumlocutions or niceties that so often paper over or obscure the real issue. Agitating requires close listening and then posing specific and sometimes tough questions aimed at getting to the deeper issue or frustration. At its best, it provokes honesty while providing a safe space to express one's true interests, anger, and point of view. It may also heighten tension with the intent of defining more clearly what is at stake and what the opposing sides of the disagreement are. In this way, these techniques promote candid dialogue, a practice of utmost importance for fostering a deep relational culture. For just as with any committed relationship, deep and healthy relationships are forged through the process of working out conflicts. This is even more important, we think, for a community of disciples as they seek together to grow to embody Jesus Christ.

The rule of Christ also integrates attentive engagement in a listening culture (described in chapter five) and its process of communal discernment, important to the ongoing dynamic life and mission of the church. From this point of view, then, conflict becomes "socially useful" because it offers the community an opportunity to "attend to new data from new perspectives."[9] Active congregations necessitate such a practice of collective discernment, as this process not only provides them a means of learning how to go forward when the way is not completely clear but also imbues them with confident creativity in their active pursuit of faithfulness to the way of Jesus within their present context. Learning to face disagreement and conflict opens the gate to more active commitment and involvement, invigorating the congregation by allowing it to participate more fully in the bountiful work of God.

The Rule of Christ in Practice

Having defended the absolute significance of the rule of Christ in the practices of an organizing body, what does it look like in *actual* practice? The practice of community (re)formation as a process of binding and loosing is both gritty and hopeful. Too often, expectations of reconciliation are naïve to the reality of community dynamics and human relations or are met with swift judgments of utopianism or idealism. But we have learned that by engaging in the hard work of binding and loosing with a deep commitment to the process rather than simply expecting idealistic outcomes, our community has been greatly strengthened (and made more honest), especially when the work of reconciliation and discernment has been lengthy and outcomes far less than ideal. The work has also greatly deepened the relational fabric of our congregation while mobilizing us to actively engage wider, and riskier, missional opportunities.

Let's recall again how deeply impactful the 2008 financial crisis, partly triggered by subprime home mortgage lending, was for the lives of Americans. Retirement savings were devastated. A tidal wave of home foreclosures ensued. The following spring, the Industrial Areas Foundation (IAF) along with NC Power (its North Carolina statewide organization) began to organize for action against corporate greed and exploitative lending practices. The primary targets were lending and foreclosure practices of multinational banks, primarily Bank of America and Wells Fargo because of their substantial holdings and the fact that their corporate headquarters were located in North Carolina. Research discovered that these banks were profiteering on predatory payday loans, charging hidden or deceptive fees, and hiking interest rates on credit cards.

Dan and I, along with several other congregants at Emmaus Way, were deeply involved in the leadership of NC Power's developing campaign against "usury," seeking to curb the banks' exploitative practices and reduce interest rates, under the banner of "10% is Enough." This multipronged action sought to publicize and hold major banks accountable for a range of unscrupulous mortgage lending practices, aggressive and insensitive foreclosure proceedings, and their heavy investiture in profitable but regressive financial instruments such as payday lending. The keynote of the campaign was a call for return to pre-Reagan era caps for credit card interest rates at 10 percent.

We felt strongly that we needed to stand with our partners in Durham CAN and NC Power in a call for institutional change and for help to those suffering under the effects of the crisis and bank policies. But even within our progressive congregation, this sentiment was not universally shared. Given that such disagreements about controversial issues pervade all congregations, this is exactly where we often falter and fall short of active and meaningful mission. Sadly, church mission often avoids initiatives that have such a sharp and provocative edge. Duke sociologist Mark Chaves, in his research on American congregations, confirms that most churches' social missions trend toward noncontroversial projects, such as disaster relief, soup kitchens, and the development of human necessities, rather than substantive social change.[10]

Of course, all of those programs are essential! But important social issues that do not generate a consensus in faith communities are typically met with inaction. Various economic viewpoints populate our congregation, and there was not complete agreement about how to go forward in the face of these issues, especially amidst the greatest financial disaster this generation had ever seen. In other words, although everyone in the community lamented the devastating impact of the financial collapse, there was certainly not a consensus that the 10 percent goal was economically reasonable or appropriate. We also had varying degrees of sensitivity and exposure to the issues of systemic poverty and racism in our culture, and, therefore, diverse notions of institutional and individual responsibility. Once again, there would be variation rather than consensus in our community regarding the significance of organizing for this work.

Dan and I both blogged and wrote about our work for the campaign, which included attending a statewide, pastor-led action in Charlotte, North Carolina, in the headquarters of Bank of America and Wells Fargo, as well as an action attending as proxies at the shareholders meeting for Bank of America to speak about mortgage relief and present the CEO (who received a $15 million dollar bonus in that meeting) with the documents of one of many customers who could not receive a response from Bank of America in regards to a legitimate request to negotiate terms. In response to our writing there was great support, but many pastors lamented their inability to join this work because of the controversy in their churches over confronting prominent businesses in our state by name or challenging profits made in the free market. Others were simply uneasy with the tactics of confrontation by collective groups gathered to garner greater voice in the debate. This is a strong testimonial to the depth of conflict aversion and the accumulation of privilege within churches in our culture. Sadly, this produces an environment in which consensus becomes a necessary antecedent to mission.

In our situation, the commitment to the rule of Christ allowed us to proceed in organizing and protest despite our internal dialogue regarding the best course of action to address corporate financial practices. As explained, the rule of Christ is highly committed to a process that works toward reconciliation rather than finding a singular outcome that defines the will of God. Resisting legalism, the practice remains somewhat flexible, recognizing that communities are constantly encountering new contexts and new information, and thus are regularly adjusting their posture to be faithful, reconciled, and missional in a changing society. In other words, there never is a fixed, static, and known will of God that must be found, proclaimed, and ratified by all in the ongoing life of the church. Practicing the rule of Christ does not seek to defend God in the world. Instead, it seeks to be faithful to the mission of Christ and reconciled to those who seek the same faithfulness.

To be faithful followers of the rule, we bound ourselves to open dialogue about the issue. We welcomed the voices of some who had cautions about the campaign into the public discourse. In this vein, we encouraged the establishment of a co-authored community blog by friends who had opposite viewpoints on finance reform. We were careful to acknowledge that at least one of our congregants who preferred restraint was a Ph.D. in corporate finance and should be heard as an expert within the community. On the other hand, when Dan and I were challenged by a few others in the community that, as theologians, we should only speak with any authority on "religious matters," we held firm to our understanding of the integration of God's work with the whole of society and our commitment to our faith being public, not simply a privatized conviction.

Our weekly pub group, which is an open forum on politics, theology, and current issues, read articles weekly on related issues. In binding ourselves to this full and open process, we found ourselves loosed by the *whole* community to participate and lead in this action. The rule of Christ allowed us to see ourselves always as leaders and as a community that is becoming rather than having arrived. Dan and I were not seeking to impose our vision authoritatively, and the community knew so. We were seeking to be faithful to the calling of our discipleship and inviting the church to join us in this discipleship as participants, prayerful supporters, and voices of advocacy and caution. Our careful application of the rule of Christ allowed the diversity of our community, and the inevitable frictions that come with diversity, to help propel us into a more thoughtful engagement with this campaign, and our whole church was blessed by an initiative many fellowships would have avoided.[11]

Juxtaposed to that positive story that affirms the rule of Christ, we can share many stories of how we have failed in its practice or are currently still hopefully working the process, with reconciliation apparently far in the future–the embodiment of this rule always continues on in search of a better harmony and peace. These negative stories, perhaps, affirm the rule even more demonstrably than the obvious successes. Our most painful stories, however, are still accounts of avoidance, when we fell prey to some of the very avoidance strategies we illustrated early in this chapter.

We had one dear friend who came to our community with many obvious gifts of leadership and service. She was wonderfully engaging and quickly became highly significant to the leadership of the community. We loved "doing church" with her, and it was hard to imagine the absence of her passion for mission and justice. From early on, we tried to imagine ways to bring her onto our staff. But it was also easy to recognize a pattern of brokenness in her relationships, deep wounds in her life story that played out with intimidation and anger toward others. Her friendship group always seemed to be shrinking, and she commonly asked us to bless her exclusions. In a community committed to relational hospitality and dialogue, conversations, negotiations, and imaginative planning, we were constantly having to circuitously avoid her larger-than-life presence. We sometimes tried covering for her and cleaning up the frustration and anger that seemed to accumulate around her. At other times, we simply avoided engaging the rule of Christ, even when we knew it was necessary for our integrity and the health of the community. And I'm sure we selfishly took advantage of her at times. She was a significant voice in our dialogue and was also leading an important community partnership initiative with some key relationships in the broader community. Either out of overoptimistic hopefulness, the instrumental need of her skills, or simple fear of conflict, we waited too long to intentionally and courageously practice the politics of forgiveness. Eventually, we did patiently and lovingly initiate the work of reconciliation with some positive outcomes. Dan, myself, and our whole leadership community learned a powerful lesson on the deep significance of the rule—regarding the personal and communal dangers of delaying its execution—a lesson we carry to this day that continually motivates us to not repeat this fearful or foolish error. We eventually learned to care for her (and, in turn, others) at our own disadvantage, willing to lose our close relationships so that she could move away from Durham on her own terms. And, indeed, she found a very engaging faith community and apparently entered this community with a willingness to engage some of the anger and wounds that she had brought to Emmaus Way. We are hopeful that this seemingly healthy landing was partially due to our practicing, albeit late, the rule of Christ. Of course, we failed in this relationship. But when a community is committed to this rule, failure is deemed as a temporary stopping place in a never-ending movement toward reconciliation.

As humans, we have differences. We certainly fail each other at times. The finite human condition is one marked by conflict and a lack of clarity. But instead of fearing conflict or feeling ill-equipped to deal with it, we have learned—both joyfully and the hard way—that working through conflict is where the church is most itself and where it can be at its best. And churches that learn to develop this skill, as James McClendon suggests, will not find it hard to expand and extrapolate from it in ways that can serve their wider society.[12]

This point of challenge can be for us a unique opportunity, embodying a process in these instances that allows us to grow in our relationships and in our understanding of what it means to be faithful in times of change. True, we could believe Jesus had no idea what he was doing when he invested his disciples with the power to bind and loose. But then again, we might ask what would be the impact on the church and on our society if we were to regain this practice? We think such a practice, to which we have returned in part through our involvement in organizing, would be quite reinvigorating and revolutionary. Embracing it and learning to embrace conflict, we can develop active congregations no longer stuck in maintenance mode or held captive by the limited agenda of one person. The intimacy that comes from relentlessly and graciously addressing conflict allows us to engage deeper in and embody more fully the reconciling, dynamic mission of God's kingdom on this earth.

7

RE-DISCOVERING the Church: An Organizing and Reorganizing Community

Graham Greene's *The Power and the Glory* describes the circuitous journey of an unnamed "whisky priest" in Mexico during the 1930s, an era of violent suppression of the Catholic Church by the government. The aptly named priest, a man who has failed his vows in many ways, seeks to flee his province, where Catholicism has been deemed entirely illegal and a certain death sentence awaits him if captured. He eventually makes it to a provincial border. But the duty of his office and the grave responsibility of being the only conduit for the salvific Eucharist, even for this man who has failed so often, drives him back from this safe haven to the city where his greatest peril lies. He returns a changed character, no less flawed but in an entirely different identity shaped by his experiences.

We (the authors) are easy marks for there-and-back, transformative stories of discovery and recovery, whether they are great stories like Greene's classic and J.R.R. Tolkien's epics or sappy Sunday night movies. We remain hopeful pastors who believe in transformation on both individual and social levels. This book began in the dual tension of disappointment and hope. We expressed our profound disappointment in the church's common absence in transformative, emancipatory social change and in its historical complicity in injustices that need to be righted. But we have also always been deeply rooted in hope of recovery. We continue to believe in the transformative social power of communities committed to a vision of Jesus' way and teaching. This text has taken us from that initial tension into a theological conversation about the sociocultural context of the contemporary church and, most importantly, into a series of specific organizing practices that we believe are transformative within the inner spiritual lives of faith communities, and are transformative to the localities that are home to these same churches. This brings us squarely back to our hopes, returning to our point of origination as changed persons of faith, renewed leaders, and participants in transformed communities of faith.

This final chapter speaks to the nature of this return and the reality of that hope. Our pastoral experience cautions us to be more specific about the quality of this hope. We have often counseled and offered spiritual direction to persons in our care who have mislabeled the hopeful aspects of their lives. Hope can be lost easily within a confluence of wounds or struggles. And, in times of challenge or pain, a hope can be misidentified as simply another component of struggle. A collaborative, realistic renaming of a person's life narrative and context is often the heart of pastoral care.

Hope is essential to organizing bodies; it informs the very identities of these communities and their leaders. Hence, we want to name intentionally some of the hopes and realities of an organizing body. Such a congregation hopes ultimately to collaboratively construct real social changes in the world, beginning in its own place, which align with Jesus' kingdom vision of justice and peace. Doing so requires and yields profound, hopeful transformations in the identities of its pastors and leaders, as well as within the character of the body itself. We are describing a hopeful dynamic that is integrative for both the leader(s) and the community.

As a "born and bred" North Carolina boy, I (Tim) grew up under the gentle tutelage of Sherriff Andy Taylor of the fictional Mayberry, North Carolina, played by our iconic native Andy Griffith, in the classic black-and-white TV show that carried his name. In the eternal wisdom of Andy, which played out in countless episodes, you could "go off to the big city," "put on airs," or even truly make yourself a better person, but Mayberry would always be waiting for you— unchanged in its values and way of life. The clear implication was that you were, no matter how substantively you grew or regressed personally in another more urban location, always the best version of yourself when returning to the safe, constant, unassailable values of home. This is not the assumption in organizing. Organizing assures not only changed and changing leaders and individuals, but also changed and changing home communities in actions and values. Committing to these practices assures the absence of a static church community, substituting instead a context of perpetual dynamism. To that, the good folks in Mayberry might say, "Heaven help us." Living in a dynamic of change would be horrifyingly unacceptable in Mayberry, and is, indeed, frightful for many leaders and congregations. But there is a beauty to this reality that has everything to do with the unquenchable Spirit of God and an ever-striving toward the realization of a living shalom on this earth. And despite all the mythology that imagines some near or distant utopian season of Christendom in the U.S., the Christian church in our society does not have an idyllic past. However, we do believe it can have a beautiful future, so we press on, working toward that hopeful horizon.

Organizing and Reorganizing

This declaration of a kinetic community, ever changing and evolving, should not come as a surprise. We have certainly not described or advocated for a church template. Instead, we have recommended a process, a constellation of ongoing practices, a way of living in the church that yields significant and perpetual transformations. In a speech to the Student Non-Violent Coordinating Community (SNCC), Cesar Chavez tried to distinguish his work from that of a typical labor leader. He explained, "When you read of labor organizing in this country, you can say there is a point where labor is 'organized.' But in community organizing, there never is a point where you can say, 'It is organized.'"[1] The organizing principles we are proposing envision a dynamic community, a church or faith community that is perpetually organizing and reorganizing. This feels entirely right to us, because the Spirit of God is never static and cannot be predicted, planned, or charted by any human algorithm. As he was with the disciples after his resurrection, Jesus is present with us and ahead of us (Mt. 26:32). The result is a beautiful, messy, complicated, and meaningful church life that is open-ended, adventuresome, creative, and transformative to the world around it.

We hope that we have added a great deal of specific practices related to the type of organizing and reorganizing that is characteristic of a church dynamically committed to listening to its internal community, learning from its social context, and living as an emancipatory partner in that social context. But we also want to acknowledge that the concept of organizing can provoke radically different images and involve equally distinct types of actions. I (Tim) should confess now that I am one of those insufferable neatnik, everything-in-its-place types. Similarly, I know Dan usually begins writing by cleaning his room, the fridge, and anything else that tends to regularly return to clutter and disorder. For both of us, an organized space is a necessary prerequisite for getting down to work. We both also tend to work on one project at a time and are highly linear in our progression. Anyone who knows us can attest to the fact that we are terrible multitaskers. Hence, we both can get easily stuck when projects bog down or needed collaboration is delayed.

For me (Tim), this mystifies my spouse, who is capable of working on a dozen projects effectively at the same time. She is innately intuitive about opportunities and priorities, and hence always seems to be working on the most important task—while I proceed through my linear progressions. When one project bogs down, she just moves with undismayed intensity to another. She prefers a neat space, but can absolutely get it done in the midst of complete chaos. I am, by predisposition I fear, a planner. She has the proclivity to be a searcher. Our advocacy of a continual organizing and reorganizing in faith and church settings is aligned far more toward "searching" than "planning." In other words, as a leader, you are pursuing opportunities or urgencies with a fervor appropriate to the issue rather than painstakingly crafting lengthy, costly, comprehensive strategic plans that are out of date by the time they are completed and thus are continually being revised or replanned by necessity.

William Easterly defines planners as persons who seek to create large, abstract, one-size-fits-all, meta-solutions for social issues in diverse localities. In contrast, searchers recognize the diversity of localities and forge responses to social issues collaboratively with those who are the recipients of their efforts.[2] Here are Easterly's definitions in length:

> Planners raise expectations but take no responsibility for meeting them; Searchers take responsibility for their actions.
>
> Planners determine what to supply; Searchers find out what is in demand.
>
> Planners apply global blueprints; Searchers adapt to local conditions.

Planners at the top lack knowledge of the bottom;
Searchers find out what the reality is at the
bottom.

Planners never hear whether the planned get what
is needed; Searchers find out if the customer is
satisfied.

A Planner thinks he already knows the answers;
he thinks of poverty as a technical engineering
problem that his answers will solve. A Searcher
admits he doesn't know the answers in advance;
he believes that poverty is a complicated tangle
of political, social, historical, institutional, and
technological factors. A Searcher hopes to find
answers to individual problems only by trial and
error experimentation.

A Planner believes outsiders know enough to
impose solutions. A Searcher believes only
insiders have enough knowledge to find solutions,
and that most solutions must be homegrown.[3]

According to Easterly, searchers differ from planners in location
(more aligned to the bottom or local setting of an issue), expertise
(addressing concerns from the posture of a learner rather than an
informed expert), awareness of complexities (avoiding simplistic
generalizations regarding the causes of social problems) and method
(working collaboratively). In these distinctions, one likely hears
echoes of self-serving justifications of malicious enterprises, such
as colonialism, or sees the traces of large bureaucratic entities and
governing bodies in the definition of planners. One could substitute
here the difference between conquistadors and their dependence
on maps, and indigenous peoples and their connection to the
storied, living nature of space.[4] Still, we certainly do not intend
to entirely dismiss planning. There is a world stage that demands
collectives, such as bureaucracies, governments, and international
organizations, and hence there is a place for strategic planning. But
we are strongly suggesting that the inner life and missional life of
faith communities need to have a strong "searching" component
even though some bureaucracy, market branding, and strategic
planning are inevitabilities in church life.

DIPLOMATE, AMERICAN BOARD OF ORTHODONTICS

JOSEPH KUNNEL, D.D.S., M.S. M.S., PHD.
ORTHODONTIST
OFFICE HOURS BY APPOINTMENT

MORELAND BLDG
WLER AVE., SUITE 401
LINOIS 60077

(847) 675-5590 OFFICE
(847) 675-8270 FAX
kunnel.dental@gmail.com

Margaret

HAS AN APPOINTMENT ON

☐ MONDAY

☐ TUESDAY

☐ WEDNESDAY

☐ THURSDAY

☐ FRIDAY

☒ SATURDAY

DATE 11/4/17

TIME 12:00 pm

TO KEEP APPOINTMENT
24 HOURS NOTICE

A commitment to searching, to organizing and reorganizing, correlates to the construction of significantly changed identities of both leaders and the churches or faith communities they lead. Before describing those identity transitions, let's first consider a critical concept of how identities are formed, and then look specifically at the identities of organizing leaders and churches.

Identities, Communities, and Local Spaces of Practice

Over the past few centuries, many thinkers have commonly tended to consider identities, particularly personal identities, as fixed and largely independent from relationships and social contexts. The mainstream of Christianity has long been aligned with this type of thinking. Christians might describe themselves or others as saved, born again, unsaved, elect, reprobate, backslidden, mature, anointed, heretical, blessed, and any of a number of spiritual designations that are highly focused on the individual's personal relationship with God. Similarly, they might offer a fixed identity designation for church communities—such as conservative, mainline, traditional, or megachurch—with minimal acknowledgment of other ever-changing social contexts that impact these fellowships or the hybridity and fluidity of those who populate them. Certainly, many believe in concepts of conversion, progressive sanctification, and moral failure. But even these changes in status are often conceived as a movement from one fixed status to another: "Once I was lost, but now I am found." And our theological landscape has some major streams that assert the permanence of saints—that one's spiritual status can become irrevocably fixed or, as commonly said, "Once saved, always saved." All of this nomenclature and discourse serve to reinforce the common presupposition of fixed, static, or rarely changing identities.

However, in recent decades, thoughts on identities have begun to change significantly. One radical shift of many has been emphasized by major theorists such as Pierre Bourdieu and Michel de Certeau: the formative role of practice or the agency of personal actions in the construction of identities.[5] Similarly, gender theorist Judith Butler, writing on the performance of gender identities, has offered a timely and memorable illustration of the importance of agency and performance in the construction of identities.[6] Clearly, our personal identities are contingent on or shaped by our actions. Since our actions are ever changing, this change in thought implies a level of fluidity in our identities. Then, when one considers that often greater forces (such as racism) or other social structures (such as political or economic systems) can restrict the possibilities of our actions, and can do so with varying amounts of power in differing social contexts, personal identities can become even more fluid and contingent depending on where we are and what forces are acting upon us. Cultural anthropologist Dorothy Holland has written powerfully on that last idea, describing the essential role that local spaces (where practices or actions occur) play in the construction of our personal or intimate identities.[7] In local spaces, such as within a biological family, historical struggles (for example, the impact of historical racism impacting a person of color in a white family, or a strong history of abuse/alcoholism in an extended family), powerful structural constraints (such as laws that determine who can and cannot marry), and our imaginations (perhaps a sense of what a perfect family should be, derived from various media) all collide, affecting or, in some cases, determining actions that powerfully inform identities in specific settings. And, of course, we all live in multiple social locations (work, families through marriage or partnership, neighborhoods, etc.), which further complicates identity. But according to Holland, our personal or intimate identities can still be somewhat durable, especially given the significance of some of the local spaces we inhabit.[8]

The key and basic summary that emerges from this complex shift in theoretical understanding called social practice theory is that our identities as persons are neither fixed nor singular, but instead are constantly being constructed by practice in local spaces. If one takes a moment to digest this summary, one can see its immense correlation to the content of this book and its recommendations. The heart of our presentation has been on transformative practices applied in the local space of the church, a space we have named and located as potentially immensely formative on the imaginations and possibilities of personal lives. Practices, in settings such as churches and faith communities, can be powerfully decisive on personal and collective identities. Let's now consider the impacts of the practices we have advocated for on the identities of leaders and the community itself. Therein lie the great hope of our recommendations and the balm for the disappointments that generated this book.

Leaders as Pastoral Ethnographers, Liturgists of Lament, and Co-conspirators in the Work of Social Justice

In the space of a church practicing solidarity with the poor, the recognition of gifts (the "fullness of Christ"), and the politics of forgiveness (the "rule of Christ"), the identities of its pastoral leaders have the possibility of profound renegotiation and relocation.[9] A seemingly endless number of pastoral identities are available for leaders. We won't attempt to rehearse an inexhaustive list of positive and negative possibilities. But with such significance placed on spaces, locations, geographies, and communities, pastoral leaders will certainly need to become far more attuned to their surroundings, the histories of their local communities, the structures of power that create and protect injustices around them, and the key local spaces that impact identities in their congregations.

With these growing sensitivities and studies, we envision pastoral leaders embracing an identity as pastoral ethnographers as a vital complement to their other roles as teachers, caregivers, and leaders. In fact, we imagine all these staple roles being deeply impacted by an ethnographic practice. Ethnography is a method of research that relies heavily on observation by deep personal engagement, the study of histories, intentional listening within communities, and the careful or artful writing of stories about communities that are studied. In recent decades, the ideal of ethnographic practice has become inextricably entwined with the work of social justice, liberation from oppression, and emancipation.[10] There is clear synchronicity between the practices of ethnography (such as observation by deep personal engagement or intentional listening), its presuppositions regarding the role of power in social contexts, its justice-saturated aspirations, and the recommended practices of this book. The pastoral setting, particularly congregations seeking to organize for greater social justice, is a natural fit for ethnographic practice. And, indeed, we heartily expect this to become a key identity for organizing pastors and leaders. Relational meetings, listening sessions, the politics of forgiveness, the acknowledgment of (oppressive or liberative) power in all community settings, and greater proximity to the poor and vulnerable will all demand ethnographic wisdom and impose an ethnographic identity for key leaders.

One might think that such a practiced study of places, histories, and communities would be normal for pastoral leaders. Theologian Willie Jennings once commented to me (Tim), "All pastors, of course, should be ethnographers." But in his teaching and writing, he sadly acknowledges that too many leaders serve without any detailed knowledge of the histories of the communities, lands, or buildings that are home to their churches. Too often, clergy and leaders serve in detachment from the stories of their communities and hence follow an abstract gospel doctrine that separates belief from bodies and histories. This abstraction of ministry from bodies, geographies, and histories is an enduring crisis, because these histories greatly determine the needs, injustices, or heroic possibilities that are the very fabric of the gospel incarnate within a community.

For example, let's apply a pastoral ethnographic gaze to the church Dan and I led together. We have already shared a bit about the history of the building we rent. Let's consider the politics of our geographical location. Our church meets a mile west of the main vertical dividing roads of our city, Mangum Street / Roxboro Street. We are located near the Brightleaf community of tobacco warehouses that have been converted into upscale housing just two blocks from Duke University's east campus, and two blocks north of the Durham freeway. Being a mile west of Mangum/Roxboro maps us on the historically "white side of town." The second descriptor, the Brightleaf neighborhood, places us inside the primary area of explosive upscale growth in Durham and in close proximity to Duke University, whose roots of plantation-style relations to the wider community continue now in the vast inequities in development and the disbursement of public resources. The Durham freeway gives us generous egress from the city, and makes it easy for people in the neighboring communities of Chapel Hill, Raleigh, and the Research Triangle Park to attend. However, the history of the freeway has its own vicious racial and socioeconomic valence. Its construction decimated a thriving black middle-class community near N.C. Central University. The severed portion to the north became part of a now enlarged low-income community that saw its property values decline further, with a diminishing of all the associated city services, plus heightened crime.

Our location is part of a greater story, as is true of every geographical setting. Our location narrates what we struggle against, who we're struggling to become, and whom people expect us to be. For our congregation, our geographical context places us deep inside a racial narrative that's often obscured or forgotten in our rapidly expanding, highly diverse, liberal, progressive, "tolerant" community. This history, and our knowledge of it, frames, interrogates, and shapes every aspect of our organizing and what it means to embody the gospel in this community. The identity shift of leaders shaped by organizing encourages us to be pastoral ethnographers, helping us "see" this story and its powerful presence in configuring the vital context in which we organize.

Joining this study of histories, geographies, and communities with the practices of organizing recommends a second identity shift for organizing pastors–becoming liturgists of lament. Our location reveals much to lament in our own history. In many senses, a ministry that is sensitive to the ubiquitous presence of power, a ministry of relentless relationship, intentional listening, and practicing the politics of forgiveness engages not only local stories but also larger historical realities of struggle and failure by the Christian church.

The work of critical theological scholars of race reveals ever so vividly how the abstraction of the gospel from localities is part of a much larger, shameful narrative. Indeed, as Willie Jennings observes, this detachment of gospel and church from bodies, lands, and animals was the dominant theological move of the colonial era that ultimately justified the economics of colonialism, the optics of race, and the ownership/enslavement of people with certain types of bodies.[11] A distorted and self-serving theological understanding of creation out of nothing ("ex nihilo") opened the door to separating people from the lands of their origin and gave permission to operate with dominion over colonized territories–often by introducing animal species, plants, and practices that were destructive to these places and the lives of the people in them. An associated theology deploying Christ's preexistence to establish God's ownership of the human, material world combined with an expansive view of the church as both the agent of salvation and the cultural locus of that salvation allowed for the seizing, trafficking, and commodification of humans if done under the banner of the church's mission of salvation.[12]

An awareness of this shameful, historical perversion of the gospel allows us to see present cooptations–namely, political and economic agendas driven by corporate profit, xenophobia, racism, competition, and individualism: all deeply defended by a skewed account of the Christian gospel. So powerful is the hold of the fear generated by these distorted versions of the gospel that real alternatives of just and peaceful living are, from the get-go, dismissed as unreasonable or even impossible. An essential element of organizing to build these alternatives is first crafting liturgies of lament to inform the worship and lives of those we lead. Critical scholars of race and culture who seek to expose the privileged position of whiteness echo this point in asserting the importance of acknowledging complicity with unjust systems as a precursor to just action.[13] In this respect, organizing pastors need to become companions with various practices of lament. This is an identity/ practice shift for leaders that requires great courage and resolve. We serve in a cultural context that demands "bold" pronouncements of certainty, happy and triumphant music, and "practical" teaching (usually defined as pithy advice that reinforces our often culturally informed–rather than biblically inspired–beliefs or aspirations). In the face of these deep, tidal flows, leaders have to not only vulnerably author this lament at times but also regularly organize and protect space for it to occur in the regular life of the body. In our own setting, the bold patronization and affirmation of our artists, allowing them to perform music in our worship liturgy that could otherwise be easily rejected for fear of offending these voracious appetites for certainty, triumphalism, and personal reinforcement, have offered great dividends. With that freedom, artists continually find and powerfully perform unique and inspiring texts that help frame the lament and resolve of our community.

A final identity shift for organizing pastors and leaders is becoming collaborators and co-conspirators in the work of social justice. This shift draws us further into the rich biblical, theological heritage of Jesus' profound identification with the poor (Mt. 25:42–46) and his insistence that his coming initiated the jubilee of Israel (Lk. 4:16–19). Such a move naturally follows an ethnographic posture that studies communities, spaces, and histories, as well as a liturgist identity that frames responses of lament as a complement to social action. All of the practices we have advocated for strongly in this text support this ultimate identity shift for organizing leaders. The recognition of gifts (the "fullness of Christ") is profoundly respectful of humanity by declaring the created dignity of all persons and urging a mode of encounter that values the perspective of each person. Baptism marks the initiation into a new creation by compelling practitioners to imagine a new social reality devoid of past divisions and injustices. The Eucharist table of Jesus is a social action that establishes the vision of baptism by including all persons, demolishing social boundaries, and meeting essential needs of the poor. The rule of Christ requires that we live the politics of reconciliation and constantly organize and reorganize with justice in mind. All of these are practices that invoke a theo-political imagination necessarily intertwined with the historical experiences of real human struggles, such as racism, classism, and poverty. They also form leaders, congregants, and communities in the work of justice.

The rule of Christ, and its passion for process, particularly nuances our collaborative work of social justice activism along lines of essential truth-telling. We are writing during the middle of what now feels like a never-ending Presidential campaign. One of our pet peeves is the near eschatological and salvific promises of change being made by candidates of both parties. So many of these promises not only are unlikely but also are outside the constitutional purview of the office of the President. This rhetoric is not substantively dissimilar to the posture of so many pastors who have sadly taken up the mantle of certainty brokers. "If you follow [read: finance] my vision, we'll blow out the doors with growth, win this city for Christ, and overcome the forces of unbelief!" Certainly, there is much in our scripture to support boldness. But pastoral leaders rarely have any leverage to assert the probability of these outcomes with anywhere near the certainty that accompanies the proclamation. Instead, one possibility of the prevalence of this certainty discourse is tragic. My (Tim) pastoral vocation for over three decades has been dominated by care with persons in their twenties and thirties, among whom the disillusioned and those who have been burned by the church have been highly represented. The dominant reaction is the lament that they felt like victims of over-promising or even outright lies.

The rule of Christ, or the politics of forgiveness, is unequivocally a process of organizing and reorganizing rather than an assurance of an outcome. It demands the truth-telling of uncertainty (to accompany some of the gracious certainties of faith), dominated by the humility of many "I don't knows," powerfully accentuated by the embodied practices of patient love. The organizing leader no longer functions as a guarantor of results, but instead serves as a guardian to a process aligned with the teaching of Jesus. In this way, the leader becomes a protector of the processes of forgiveness, reconciliation, and love, and the curator of a community committed to enact a courageous sanctuary so that these processes can thrive. In effect, one curates a community that is perpetually organizing and reorganizing as a response to the movements of God's Spirit and the voices of its people in alignment with relentless searching for opportunities to enact God's mission of justice.

All of these identity shifts of the leader are not small shifts or easy charges to enact. But we believe they result in radically transformed and newly invigorated faith communities. As a hopeful conclusion, let's now consider identify shifts in organizing communities and congregations.

An Artistic and Adventuresome, Courageous and Joyful Church

An organizing and reorganizing church, a community of relentless searchers instead of obsessive planners, a community committed to parish and geography, and a community committed to the work of reconciliation has the beautiful possibility of becoming an artistic and adventuresome body. This is a community not paralyzed by fears of messiness, uncertainty, or change. Instead, a level of perpetual process, deliberation, and struggle is embraced. The community is held together by practices of discernment, a thick relationality, striving for reconciliation, laments of historical failures, and the embodied work of justice, rather than tightly defined and often over-promised plans and goals. A community in this posture and practice can readily become artistically beautiful and engaging. This beauty will inevitably include some of the tangles that accompany creative space formed in a responsive, listening community. But we believe such a messy, beautiful, and creative adventure is worth the ride.

When we reflect on the invitation in this book, we believe we are inviting you to a sacred terrain where the worshipful acts of courage and play are highly privileged. We are deeply indebted to the marvelous biblical exegesis of Eugene Peterson in *Working the Angles*, in which he demonstrated that in lives defined by the rhythms of worship, courage and play are by no means an odd pairing.[14] Courage is certainly required for both the intent and execution of any practice that relocates the church to stand in solidarity with the poor and vulnerable. As we have vigorously defended, the resistance to this relocation is relentless and powerful internally within churches that have been formed in histories and theologies of privilege, and externally from a culture that has been economically enriched on the backs of race and prejudice. It also takes courage for leaders to cede control to the gifting of the community, and it requires persistent and patient strength to live into the politics of forgiveness. But none of these courageous practices by any means precludes the often whimsical, adventurous, joyful, and artful posture of play.

We see and admire this combination in the Franciscan Friars of the Renewal (Bronx, New York), who photograph and chronicle their work in playful engagement with human needs. Their images of brothers skateboarding in the neighborhood, blessing buildings beside toddler "acolytes" who joyfully accompany them on big wheels, and even robed and hooded brothers playing punk rock at the Catholic Underground music festival strongly cement the joyful possibility of play with a commitment to missional courage.[15] After three years of ethnographic study and pastoral participation in the NAACP's "Forward Together" Moral Movement of Protest, we have seen this same type of joining of prophetic outrage at systemic injustice with a social movement characterized by a radical, joyful inclusiveness.

Our invitation to our readers and their communities is not for the faint of heart nor the dull of spirit. We believe these practices and logics of organizing the body provide a real pattern for generating grassroots transformations within congregations, as well as pathways to real social change in our localities. These are the aspirations, sustained practices, and unquenchable hopes we hold ourselves to in our own ministries and teaching. With us, it is still a work in progress. We're continually rediscovering the vitality of the body of Christ in the process. We haven't arrived. We aren't organized. But we are still organizing!

Appendix 1

One-to-Ones:
Building a Relational Culture

The core of building a thick relational culture is connecting to others. A one-to-one relational meeting is a proven technique for this.

What Is a One-to-One?

A one-to-one

- is an individual, relational meeting designed to establish a connection between persons and to investigate the possibility of working together in the future.

- is not visitation, not a date, not even a friendship meeting.

- is an important organizational step to reweaving the relational fabric.

- is the core and base of healthy and active ministry.

- takes time, energy, and persistence. It also takes a level of strategy.

- is an intentional conversation meant to elicit connections, personal stories for connection, and possibilities for mutual cooperation.

Goals of One-to-One

The general purpose of the one-to-one is to build and strengthen a relationship. Other goals include:

- connecting with a broader cross section of persons in or related to your ministry. Often leaders can get siloed off, and, as a result, be myopic in their view of who the ministry is or who a good leader is.

- identifying and recruiting leaders.

- modeling the values of your organization (of openness, honesty, resourcefulness, vulnerability, for example).

- modeling respectful ways of listening and sharing to discover areas of mutual commitment and import.

- using it as an entry point for more relational meetings (Especially at the beginning, it's good to meet with people who you believe have many other connections/relationships in the community).

Setting Up the Meeting

When you reach out to set up the meeting, you should let the person know why you want to meet with her/him. As with all requests, the person can negotiate a response; they may say no, yes, or modify or ask questions that help strengthen the purpose of the meeting and the relationship. It is important to be *as clear with yourself as you can* before making the request and to be open and respectful of the needs and time constraints of the person you hope to meet with.

Once you are clear about the purpose, as well as your hoped-for outcomes, of the meeting, choose the most appropriate way to set it up. Rule of thumb: personal is always best.

Be organized, ready, and prompt. One-to-one meetings should last about thirty minutes. People will appreciate your preparation, as well as the sense of purpose you bring to the meeting. (This does not mean being rude or failing to listen, as we will see, but it does mean that you have a plan and sense of direction for the conversation. You're not just dillydallying!!!) Be sure to manage the time but also be flexible.

Steps of a One-to-One Meeting

I. Opening/ Credential

Start out by giving your credential (your position and organization/congregation, the person who referred him/her to you, etc.) and briefly summarize why you want to meet.

II. Breaking the Ice

It doesn't work well to rush into heavy questions, such as, "What do you worry about for you and your family?" Start with something easier, such as: "How long have you been involved with _____ ministry?" or, "What kinds of things have you been involved with here?" or, "What got you interested in serving/working/ worshiping here?" or, "What brought you and your family to this church?"

III. Discover the Person's Interests and Connections

An important part of this conversation is to get a sense of what the person's interests are–that is, what things are most important to her/him and why? There are many ways to get at this, and part of learning the art of conducting a one-to-one meeting will be to develop your own style. One way is to use your own story to talk about the things you find essential and important, and then to ask the other person to share. Another is simply to ask probing questions while listening to the other person's story, questions that elicit values and commitments, such as, "Why is that important to you?" or, "Why did you want to do that?" or, "What is your vision for this ministry/organization?"

Crucial here is to figure out if the person is a doer or complainer. To do this, when a sensitive area comes up, ask permission to inquire more on the topic. Then you may "agitate" around this theme to see how thoughtfully the person reacts by asking, "What have you done about this?" or, "Why haven't you done something about this?" or, "Are you ready to do something about this?"

IV. Closing and Proposal of Next Steps

After you've learned more about this person, decide if there are points of connection and mutual commitment. Then propose some next step. It may be as simple as asking, "After I talk to some other people, can we talk again?" Or you may ask the person to come with you to meet with others or take part in some action related to a shared central concern.

V. Evaluation

Afterward, spend a few minutes reflecting on the meeting. Ask yourself:

1. Is this person a leader? What is her/his potential to become a leader? What about this person's story, actions, thoughtfulness, passion, or anger makes me think this or not?

2. What is more important to this person? What is she/he willing to take action on?

3. Who is this person connected to in positive (and negative) ways? Is there anyone I think this person should meet?

4. How did I do in the one-to-one? What questions should I have asked that I didn't?

Appendix 2

House Meetings/Listening Sessions: Building a Relational Culture

What Are House Meetings/Listening Sessions?

Listening sessions are succinct and directed meetings of eight to twelve persons organized for the purpose of bringing people together to tell their stories, identify areas of mutual commitment and concern, and build shared identity through congealing hopes, desires, frustrations, and possibilities for action. (They are NOT a dinner club or a time to show off your home/ office, a bitch session, an inquisition).

What Are the Goals of a House Meeting?

• To elicit personal stories and build solidarity

• To identify areas of shared concern or import or common frustrations and concerns

• To build a mutual vision

• To identify leaders

• To propose new actions by discerning possible ways forward

Hosting a House Meeting

Because house meetings are intentional and purposeful gatherings, you should come prepared with some specific questions that are broad in nature, but ask people to articulate their stories and interests in connection with the ministry or organization.

One of your key jobs (as in the one-to-one meeting) is to probe the initial answers people provide in order to try to get at the root of what really sparks their passion–either anger or enthusiasm (and hopefully a little of both). At times this may feel like you're pushing beyond comfort level, and folks may get frustrated initially, but what you're really doing is getting them to articulate for you what they really care about, where their energy is focused. This is what we call "agitation."

It's important to take notes during the process, as the ideas, topics, issues, and stories that come out in the house meeting will be raw data for you going forward. (You may consider recording it on your phone if you want and then going back to take your notes).

Identify leaders. We are also keen to locate folks who show a strong sense of passion around things and might be tapped to lead specific initiatives or ministry actions.

After House Meetings

Once you've engaged in a series of house meetings, the idea is that you then work to bring the data together in order to see places of overlap. Are there areas of shared concern or frustration? What similarities in the stories have emerged? Are there shared hopes for the future? Are there common commitments that are not being tapped? Are there new persons with giftings we are not currently recognizing that may really help us here? Overall, does this tell us anything about our organization/ministry and its direction, especially in light of what the people connected with it think?

Notes

Chapter 1: RE-Assessing the Church

1 Lyrics from "The Long Defeat" by Sara Groves, copyright ©2007 Sara Groves Music (admin. by Music Services). All rights reserved. ASCAP.

2 Quoted in A. Billingsley and C.H. Caldwell, "The Church, the Family, and the School in the African American community," *The Journal of Negro Education,* vol. 60, no. 3 (1991): 427–40.

3 For example, see Tim Conder, "In God's Country: Deploying Detournement to Expose the Enmeshment of Christianity within the Spectacle of Capitalism," in *Detournement as Pedagogical Praxis,* ed. Jim Trier (Rotterdam, The Netherlands: Sense Publishers, 2014), 129–54.

4 See Stanley Hauerwas and William Willimon, *Resident Aliens: Life in the Christian Colony, A Provocative Christian Assessment of Culture and Ministry for People Who Know That Something Is Wrong* (Nashville: Abington Press, 2014), and Rodney Clapp, *A Peculiar People: The Church as Culture in a Post-Christian Society* (Downers Grove, Ill.: InterVarsity Press, 1996).

5 The NAACP's "Forward Together" Moral Movement has arisen in the wake of a sharp return to the old Southern politics of voter suppression, racial exclusion, prejudice, and vilification of the poor in North Carolina. The courage and joy of this movement are embodied by its convening leader, the Rev. Dr. William Barber, North Carolina's NAACP president, who brings a visible, childlike joy at the moving of God's Spirit to his booming voice of moral outrage. The heart of his message was dramatically on display in his plenary speech at the 2016 Democratic National Convention. To read more about this beautiful uprising of jubilee justice, see William J. Barber with Barbara Zelter, *Forward Together: A Moral Message for the Nation* (St. Louis: Chalice Press, 2014) and William J. Barber with Jonathan Wilson-Hartgrove, *The Third Reconstruction: Moral Mondays, Fusion Politics, and the Rise of a New Justice Movement* (Boston: Beacon Press, 2016).

6 Our team represented the Clergy Caucus of Durham Congregations, Associations, and Neighborhoods (CAN). CAN, like BUILD, is a local organization

affiliated with the Industrial Areas Foundation (IAF): "Founded in 1940, the Industrial Areas Foundation is the nation's largest and longest-standing network of local faith and community-based organizations" (retrieved from industrialareasfoundation.org). Many of the narratives of successful organizing in this book are derived from our work and affiliation with IAF.

7 Thanks to Reverend Jim Honig for this image.

8 As Christian pastors, we are writing about the unique potential of the Christian Church to organize and impact our society given its own historical narrative and its gospel. But of course, other faith traditions and ethical traditions have deep commitments to justice and their own logics that drive them in this trajectory. We are confident of the power of the practices we recommend in this book in other faith and ethical traditions. The organizing we have participated in and led has always been ecumenical and multi-tradition. For readers outside of the Christian tradition, you may want to skip chapter 2, which intentionally defends the Christian theological logic for the work of justice. We are deeply confident that readers in other traditions can supply their own rationale to support the practices we accentuate and we eagerly look forward to collaborative dialogue with them.

Chapter 2: RE-Defining the Church

1 Peter L. Berger, "The Desecularization of the World: A Global Overview," in *The Desecularization of the World: Resurgent Religion and World Politics,* ed. Peter L. Berger (Grand Rapids, Mich.: William B. Eerdmans Publishing Company, 1999), 18.

2 John D. Zizioulas, *Being as Communion: Studies in Personhood and the Church* (Crestwood, N.Y.: St. Vladimir's Seminary Press, 1985), 131–32.

3 Robert W. Jenson, *Systematic Theology, Volume 2: The Works of God* (Oxford, U.K.: Oxford University Press, 1999), 179.

4 James W. McClendon Jr., *Ethics: Systematic Theology, Volume 1,* 2d ed. (Waco, Tex.: Baylor University Press, 2012), 19.

5 Alena Hall, "Why Working the Night Shift Has Major Health Consequences," *Huffington Post,* January 6, 2015 (updated April 24, 2015). Accessed February 9, 2016, http://www.huffingtonpost.com/2015/01/06/rotating-shift-work-health_n_6417644.html.

6 For a more complete discussion of the notion of the "fullness of Christ," see John Howard Yoder, *The Fullness of Christ: Paul's Vision of Universal Ministry* (Elgin, Ill.: Brethren Press, 1987).

7 Zizioulas, *Being as Communion,* 114.

8 John Howard Yoder, *Body Politics: Five Practices of the Christian Community Before the Watching World* (Scottdale, Pa.: Herald Press, 2001), 21.

9 Oscar Romero, *Voice of the Voiceless: The Four Pastoral Letters and Other Statements* (Maryknoll, Md.: Orbis Books, 1985; reprint 2003), 180–81.

10 M. Shawn Copeland, *Enfleshing Freedom: Race, Body, and Being* (Minneapolis: Fortress Press, 2010), 126.

11 See Tim Conder and Daniel Rhodes, *Free for All: Rediscovering the Bible in Community* (Grand Rapids, Mich.: Baker Books, 2009).

12 Mikael Broadway, Curtis Freeman, Barry Harvey, James Wm. McClendon Jr., Elizabeth Newman, and Philip Thompson, "Re-envisioning Baptist Identity: A Manifesto for Baptist Communities in North America." Published in *Baptists Today,* (June 26, 1997) and in *Perspectives in Religious Studies* 24, no. 3 (1997): 303–10.

13 John Howard Yoder, "Practicing the Rule of Christ," in *Virtues and Practices in the Christian Tradition: Christian Ethics After MacIntyre,* ed. Nancey Murphy, Brad J. Kallenburg, and Mark Thiessen Nation (Notre Dame, Ind.: University of Notre Dame Press, 1997; reprint 2003), 143. Also, see Yoder's discussion of this practice in Body Politics, 1–13, 61–70. While he rightly saw this practice as central to the church, sadly Yoder frequently derailed and thwarted it when it came to addressing his own abusive actions. This is particularly disturbing for those of us who have been so influenced by his thought, and we hope that our reference to his writings herein does not further silence or dismiss those he victimized.

14 McClendon, *Ethics,* 225–26. In his discussion of the practice of "shaping communities," which closely resembles how we understand the practice of the rule of Christ, Larry Rasmussen states, "It is the practice that provides the choreography for all other practices of a community or society," Rasmussen, "Shaping Communities," in *Practicing Our Faith: A Way of Life for a Searching People,* ed. Dorothy C. Bass (San Francisco: Jossey-Bass, 1997), 120.

15 For a more detailed description of this open meeting, see Gayle Kountz, "Meeting in the Power of the Spirit: Ecclesiology, Ethics, and the Practice of Discernment," in *The Wisdom of the Cross: Essays in Honor of John Howard Yoder,* ed. Stanley Hauerwas, et al. (Grand Rapids, Mich.: Wm B. Eerdmans Publishing Co., 1999), 327–48.

16 Catherine Keller, *On the Mystery: Discerning Divinity in Process* (Minneapolis: Fortress Press, 2008), 115.

17 Ibid.

18 In a wonderful essay on poverty and prayer, Kelly Johnson describes how the practice of true prayer cannot be divorced from the sharing of needs and goods in a context of honest recognition and conflict resolution. Kelly Johnson, "Interceding: Poverty and Prayer," in *The Blackwell Companion to Christian Ethics,* 2d ed., ed. Stanley Hauerwas and Samuel Wells (Malden, Mass.: Wiley-Blackwell, 2011), 239–50.

19 Jenson, *Systematic Theology, Volume 2,* 170.

20 Stanley Hauerwas, *The Peaceable Kingdom: A Primer in Christian Ethics* (Notre Dame, Ind.: University of Notre Dame Press, 1983), 99.

21 Martin Luther King Jr., *Strength to Love* (Philadelphia: Fortress Press, 1981), 27.

22 McClendon, *Ethics,* 236.

23 Stuart Murray, *Post-Christendom* (Carlisle, U.K.: Paternoster, 2004), 244.

24 Rasmussen, "Shaping Communities," 125.

Chapter 3: RE-Empowering the Church

1 Saul D. Alinsky, *Rules for Radicals: A Practical Primer for Realistic Radicals* (1971; reprint, New York: Vintage Books, 1989), 3.
2 Astra Taylor, "Against Activism," *The Baffler*, No. 30 (2016), available at: http://thebaffler.com/salvos/against-activism accessed May 12, 2016.
3 Dennis A. Jacobsen, *Doing Justice: Congregations and Community Organizing* (Minneapolis: Augsburg Fortress, 2001), 43. This perspective on power is one that, for us, has also been greatly enriched by womanist critiques of power simply understood as domination. See bell hooks, *Feminist Theory: From Margin to Center* (Boston: South End Press, 1984), 83–93.
4 David Lose, "Pentecost 7B: A Tale of Two Kingdoms," July 6, 2015, available at: http://www.davidlose.net/2015/07/pentecost-7-b-a-tale-of-two-kingdoms/ accessed May 12, 2016.
5 Ched Myers, *Binding the Strongman: A Political Reading of Mark's Story of Jesus* (1988; reprint, Maryknoll, N.Y.: Orbis Books, 2008), 194.
6 Bill Easum, *Unfreezing Moves: Following Jesus into the Mission Field* (Nashville: Abingdon Press, 2001), 31–33.
7 Edward T. Chambers with Michael A. Cowen, *Roots for Radicals: Organizing for Power, Action, and Justice* (Continuum International Publishing Group, Inc., 2010; reprint, New York: Bloomsbury Academic, 2013), 28.
8 Ibid.
9 Gregory Boyle, *Tattoos on the Heart: The Power of Boundless Compassion* (New York: Free Press, 210), 188.
10 Dee Hock, "The Art of Choardic Leadership," in *On Mission and Leadership: A Leader to Leader Guide*, ed. Frances Hesselbein and Rob Johnston (San Francisco: Jossey-Bass, 2002), 65.
11 Robert Michels, *Political Parties: A Sociological Study of the Oligarchical Tendencies of Modern Democracy*, trans. Eden and Cedar Paul (New York: Collier Books, 1962).
12 Our discussion of the powers here is deeply indebted to John Howard Yoder's chapter on "Christ and the Powers," in *The Politics of Jesus: Vicit Agnus Noster*, 2d ed. (reprint, Grand Rapids, Mich.: Eerdmans Publishing Co., 2002), 134–61.

Chapter 4: RE-Connecting the Church

1 See Emily Badger, "The long, painful and repetitive history of how Baltimore became Baltimore," April 29, 2015 (available at: http://www.washingtonpost.com/blogs/wonkblog/wp/2015/04/29/the-long-painful-and-repetitive-history-of-how-baltimore-became-baltimore/ accessed January 20, 2016), for some historical perspective on the long systemic roots of poverty in Baltimore. This backdrop offers both a context for the challenge BUILD and others working for economic recovery face and of the stark beauty regarding the impact the organizing initiatives described here in light of that challenge.
2 See Wendell Berry's 1983 essay "Two Economies," anthologized in *The Art of the Commonplace: The Agrarian Essays of Wendell Berry*, ed. Norman Wirzba (Berkeley: Calif.: Counterpoint, 2002), 219–35.

3 See William Julius Wilson, *When Work Disappears: The World of the New Urban Poor* (New York: Vintage Books, 1997).

4 Robert D. Putnam, *Bowling Alone: The Collapse and Revival of American Community* (New York: Simon & Schuster, 2000).

5 Robert N. Bellah, et al., *Habits of the Heart: Individualism and Commitment in American Life* (Berkeley, Calif.: University of California Press, 2008).

6 We have described, following the lead of Bellah and colleagues, several lifestyle enclaves, such as gated neighborhoods, that are available to people at the higher end of socioeconomic status. However, this compensation to loneliness and isolation happens at every level of the socioeconomic scale, including the very lowest. See Philippe Bourgois and Jeff Schonberg's *Righteous Dopefiend* (Berkeley, Calif.: University of California Press, 2009) for a poignant and graphic detailing of intimate friendship and community formation in the very distinct enclave of heroin injectors living under the bridges and in the public spaces of San Francisco in the 1990s through the turn of the century.

7 See Paul Sparks, Tim Soerens, and Dwight J. Friesen, *The New Parish: How Neighborhood Churches are Transforming Mission, Discipleship, and Community* (Downers Grove, Ill.: InterVarsity Press, 2014).

8 See Omar McRoberts, *Streets of Glory: Church Community in a Black Urban Neighborhood* (Chicago: University of Chicago Press, 2003).

9 Hugh Heclo, *On Thinking Institutionally* (Boulder, Co.: Paradigm Publishers, 2008), 82–89.

10 Ibid., 83.

11 Christine Negroni, "Priest's Video Contradicts Police Report on Arrest," March 12, 2009, available at: http://www.nytimes.com/2009/03/13/nyregion/13harass.html?_r=0 accessed January 20, 2015.

12 Ed Jacovino, "The Rev. James Manship: 'I'm not an activist, I'm a priest,'" July 1, 2012, available at: http://www.nhregister.com/article/NH/20120701/NEWS/307019992 accessed January 20, 2015.

13 Willie James Jennings in *The Christian Imagination: Theology and the Origins of Race* (New Haven, Conn.: Yale University Press, 2010). Here Jennings powerfully connects Christian theology with colonial racism occurring under the dominant Christendom that established the modern world. "Christianity in the Western World lives and moves within a diseased social imagination," he laments (p. 6). See Jennings' chapter "Being Baptized: Race," in *The Blackwell Companion to Christian Ethics*, 2d ed., ed. Stanley Hauerwas and Samuel Wells (Malden, Mass.: Wiley-Blackwell, 2011), to read his argument in a shorter form.

Chapter 5: RE-Collecting the Church

1 William Willimon, *Pastor: The Theology and Practice of Ordained Ministry* (Nashville: Abingdon Press, 2002), 60.

2 Mark A. Throntveit, *Ezra–Nehemiah*, Interpretation Commentary Series (Louisville, Ky.: John Knox Press, 1992), 3.

3 Ibid., 11.

4 With respect to the role of these one-to-one meetings, Mark Warren has observed, "The IAF realized such meetings could help bring disconnected community residents together to talk about common concerns and develop plans of action. House meetings and individual meetings became ways to strengthen community and undertake political action–and to link the two together for mutual benefit." See Mark Warren, *Dry Bones Rattling: Community Building to Revitalize American Democracy* (Princeton, N.J.: Princeton University Press, 2001), 61.

5 Jeffrey Stout, *Blessed Are the Organized: Grassroots Democracy in America* (Princeton, N.J.: Princeton University Press, 2010), 154.

6 For those unfamiliar with the Myers-Briggs personality assessment, J stands for Judging and indicates a person who dislikes indecision and who prefers to make clear and timely verdicts rather than remaining open to new information. On the assessment scale, Js are juxtaposed to Ps, or Perceiving personalities.

7 A similar description of the process of developing the body of Christ is offered by Alexia Salvatierra and Peter Heltzel in *Faith-Rooted Organizing: Mobilizing the Church in Service to the World* (Downers Grove, Ill.: InterVarsity Press, 2014), 145–68.

8 We thoroughly recommend Samuel Wells and Marcia A. Owen, *Living Without Enemies: Being Present in the Midst of Violence* (Downers Grove, Ill.: InterVarsity Press, 2011).

Chapter 6: RE-Uniting the Church

1 For a description of the clash of civilizations, see Samuel P. Huntington, *The Clash of Civilizations and the Remaking of World Order* (New York: Simon & Schuster, 1996), and, on the discussion of culture wars, see James Davidson Hunter, *Culture Wars: The Struggle to Define America* (New York: Basic Books, 1991), and, for a discussion of social fragmentation, see Robert D. Putnam, *Bowling Alone: The Collapse and Revival of American Community* (New York: Simon & Schuster, 2000).

2 Alan Wolfe, *One Nation After All: What Middle-Class Americans Really Think About: God, Country, Family, Racism, Welfare, Immigration, Homosexuality, Work, the Right, the Left, and Each Other* (New York: Viking Press, 1998), 54.

3 See Tim Conder and Daniel Rhodes, *Free for All: Rediscovering the Bible in Community* (Grand Rapids, Mich.: Baker Books, 2009). In this text, we focused heavily on how the lack of dialogue damages the authenticity of communities.

4 Wolfe, *One Nation After All*, 54.

5 David Hollenbach, S.J., *The Common Good and Christian Ethics* (Cambridge, U.K.: Cambridge University Press, 2002), 40.

6 Saul D. Alinsky, *Rules for Radicals: A Practical Primer for Realistic Radicals* (1971; reprint, New York: Vintage Books, 1989), 62.

7 Ibid. 21.

8 Dennis A. Jacobsen, *Doing Justice: Congregations and Community Organizing* (Minneapolis: Augsburg Fortress, 2001), 69.

9 John Howard Yoder, *Body Politics: Five Practices of the Christian Community Before the Watching World* (Scottdale, Pa.: Herald Press, 2001), 8.

10 See Mark Chaves, *Congregations in America* (Cambridge, Mass.: Harvard University Press, 2004), and Mark Chaves, *American Religion: Contemporary Trends* (Princeton, N.J.: Princeton University Press, 2011).

11 A quick glance at your credit card interest agreement reveals that the campaign was not fully successful regarding credit card usury by major financial institutions. But we did receive some major concessions, holding the banks accountable for previous commitments regarding lending to the families of veterans serving overseas and significant changes in addressing the foreclosure crisis.

12 James W. McClendon Jr., *Ethics: Systematic Theology, Volume 1*, 2d ed. (Waco, Tex.: Baylor University Press, 2012), 236.

Chapter 7: RE-Discovering the Church

1 Cesar Chavez, *An Organizer's Tale: Speeches,* ed. Ilan Stevens (New York: Penguin Books, 2008), 3.

2 William Easterly, *The White Man's Burden: Why the West's Efforts to Aid the Rest Have Done So Much Ill and So Little Good* (New York: Penguin Press, 2006).

3 Ibid., 6.

4 See Walter D. Mignolo, *The Darker Side of the Renaissance: Literacy, Territoriality, and Colonization,* 2d ed. (Ann Arbor, Mich.: The University of Michigan Press, 2003), 259–313.

5 In this shift toward practice in the understanding and construction of identities, the works of French sociologist, Pierre Bourdieu, and French Jesuit, Michel de Certeau, stand out. Their classic works include Pierre Bourdieu, *Outline of a Theory of Practice,* trans. Richard Nice (Cambridge, N.Y.: Cambridge University Press, 1997), and Michel de Certeau, *The Practice of Everyday Life* (Berkeley, Calif.: University of California Press, 1984).

6 See Judith Butler, *Gender Trouble: Feminism and the Subversion of Identity* (New York: Routledge, 1990).

7 Dorothy Holland, William Lachicotte, Debra Skinner, and Carole Cain, *Identity and Agency in Cultural Worlds* (Cambridge, Mass.: Harvard University Press, 1998).

8 Ibid.

9 We are using the term "pastoral leaders" to include ordained and paid clergy as well as all forms of lay leaders in congregations and other faith communities.

10 Ethnography as a qualitative research discipline is most historically associated with anthropology, though it is now being developed in theology. Its practice has regularly included the thick observation of communities from a posture

of embedded participation, intentional listening (often through interviewing), and the study of personal histories through dairies, public documents, or other material artifacts. The roots of ethnography were deeply entwined in colonialism, but in a penitent turn, recent forms of ethnography have developed a vigorous and evolving ethic that demands emancipatory work as a primary goal of study. For an excellent explanation of this historical development and many outstanding examples of its application, see George W. Noblit, Susanna Y. Flores, and Enrique G. Murrillo, eds., *Postcritical Ethnography: Reinscribing Critique* (Cresskill, N.J.: Hampton Press, 2004).

11 Willie James Jennings, *The Christian Imagination: Theology and the Origins of Race* (New Haven, Conn.: Yale University Press, 2010).

12 Ibid., 28.

13 See Barbara Applebaum, *Being White, Being Good: White Complicity, White Moral Responsibility, and Social Justice Pedagogy* (Lanham, Md.: Lexington, 2010).

14 Eugene Peterson, *Working the Angles: The Shape of Pastoral Integrity* (Grand Rapids: Mich., Wm. B. Eerdmans, 1987), 44–58. Peterson wrote a marvelous chapter on Sabbath, in which he artfully constructs the practice of Sabbath-keeping as a worshipful orientation to God's creative rhythm offered as a life-giving example to the created world. He demonstrates how biblical witness to Sabbath was defended as an act of the spiritual discipline of prayer in Exodus 20:8–11, and as an act of the spiritual discipline of play in Deuteronomy 5:15.

15 John Mitchell, "Monks Who Play Punk," April 22, 2007, available at: http://www.nytimes.com/2007/04/22/nyregion/thecity/22monk.html?_r=0 retrieved on April 5, 2016.